CreateSpace and Kindle Self-Publishing Masterclass

The Step-by Step Author's Guide to Writing, Publishing and Marketing Your Books on Amazon.

By Rick Smith

Second Edition 2015

Preface

There are hundreds of books about Self-Publishing on Amazon, using the Createspace and Kindle platforms. So what makes this one special?

Maybe you're writing and publishing for the first time. Or maybe you've written something special and you need to know how to get it into the hands of your audience. Whatever the case, you're looking for *results*, otherwise you'll waste a lot of time and energy, and probably come away frustrated and disillusioned. You need a System.

Just like the thousands of successful independent authors now making money on Amazon, we all start from the same place. We want to write, and we want to entertain or educate others. But how do we get started, and how do we compete with the big bad world of Publishers, Agents and Best-Selling Authors?

First, let's get one thing straight: ***there's a book inside you right now.*** My job is to get it out of you, and to get you published and selling. Luckily, I know exactly how to do this, because I do it for a living.

When I started, I was just like you. I read endless books on the subject, some good (which I'll recommend later) and some dreadful. I spent lots of money on Guru Courses and Seminars, and I tried everything until eventually I developed a system that works. I discovered the important things that you need to do, and how to avoid the other stuff that's just a waste of time and effort.

Using these methods I have built a career as a successful independent author. I write, publish and market my books with two key elements at the core: Quality and Value. The majority of my titles sell hundreds of copies each month, and I'll publish at least six new books in the coming year. I'll probably never retire, because I love what I do!

I write and publish books on a variety of unrelated topics. If I have an idea about something I'm interested in, I have a formula to research my subject and deliver my manuscript to the highest possible standard, in the shortest possible time. I spend next-to-nothing on Marketing, and I drive my whole business (because that's what it is) from my home office or my local Starbucks. I collect royalties whilst I sleep, take vacations, or drink beer in the pub. I love to write, but I also love to earn!

The Self-Publishing business has given me the freedom, both in terms of time and money, to travel the world (writing and editing as I go) and hang out with really cool, interesting people in exciting and different cities.

Following the System in this book, you'll learn how to do this too. I'll give you the tool-kit you'll need to drive your writing forwards, the easy ways to manage the Amazon Publishing Platform, and the Secret Weapons that will enable you to get your books high up in Amazon's Category Rankings.

This book is around twice the size of its main competitors because of the amount of information it contains. It is, I believe, the most comprehensive guide on the market today, and to back that up I offer you my personal guarantee: If you don't achieve your ambitions as an Independent Self-Published Author within six months, please e-mail me and I will personally refund your money. You'll find my contact details at the end of the book.

On the other hand, if you like what you read and you find it useful, please leave an honest review on Amazon so that others can join our successful Author community.

Becoming an Author is a life-changing journey, and it starts with the very first step. So if you're ready to take it, let's go!

Rick Smith
London, October 2014

About the Author

Rick Smith is an International Marketing Consultant and Self-Published Independent Author. He writes on an eclectic range of Non-Fiction subjects, including Aviation, Social Science, Technology, Hypnosis, Travel, Self-Help, and Writing & Publishing. Several of his books are consistently in their Category Top-10 lists, and this book has over one hundred five-star reviews on Amazon.com.

Rick is also the publisher and author/editor of Young Adult Fiction books by Joey K, and collaborates on Business Books with renowned international Public Speakers such as Michael Jackson and Ryan Hogarth. To check out any of these books, please go to www.ricksmithbooks.com

Rick is married to Elisabeth Bigham, an accomplished Classical Pianist, and divides his time between London and Johannesburg, South Africa - "Wherever the sun is shining!"

What's In the Book?

This book contains three main Sections, covering Writing, Publishing, and Marketing your book. Each Section is further divided into the key stages and tasks that you'll need to undertake to succeed. This book will walk you through each one, with clear directions about what to do, and how and when to do it.

Writing

Choosing what to write, refining your target customers, finding profitable categories, researching your competitors, and setting up your outline, are all covered in Section One. You'll learn about the best free and paid software tools to use for your project, whether Word Processing or dedicated Author Programs, and other fantastic free software for Organising and Collating Research Material, Planning Fiction Characters, Scenes, and Plot-Lines. I'll show you the do's and don'ts that will save you lots of time and supercharge your productivity, so you'll get your book finished on schedule. You'll also learn the best approach to editing your manuscript so that your readers will truly love your book.

Publishing

In Section Two, you'll learn how to prepare your Masterpiece for publishing: as a Paperback using Createspace, and as an e-Book using Kindle Direct Publishing (KDP). Before you go to print, you'll understand all about Formatting, Pricing, and Keywords that will put your book up there alongside the best-sellers, on a level playing field. We'll explore Page Layouts, how to Design a Winning Cover, and where to go for cheap and effective help if you're struggling with any aspect of the process. I'll reveal the Secret Weapon that will enable you to publish your Paperback and E-Book without having to do the job twice, in record time. We'll walk step-by-step through the actual publishing process to make sure that nothing ever gets left behind.

Marketing & Selling

In Section Three, you'll learn what to do and what not to do when you start selling your book on Amazon. I'll demonstrate the time-wasting methods that many authors try (and many gurus teach) and give you a low-cost Marketing Strategy to get your book noticed, and your sales moving. We'll examine the importance of your Amazon Sales Page elements, and how to tune them for maximum effect, and the tactics you can use to supercharge your Search Rankings and Reviews. Finally, you'll learn how to Track your Sales and Maximise your Royalties. You need incredible impact with the least possible effort, because you'll need to get on with writing your next Masterpiece!

All you need, and all I can teach you, is contained within these pages. And where someone else is more knowledgeable about a specific topic, and I believe they can add to your skill-set, I'll recommend their book(s) with complete impartiality.

The Ground Rules: Can You Actually Write?

Hopefully you'll immediately answer a resounding *"Yes I Can!"*

Confidence in your own ability is an important part of the success formula for authors. You don't necessarily need to be gregarious and sociable, but you need to believe that you have the skills to write informative or entertaining language for your audience, and the balls to put it out there and see what happens!

9

English is by far the most spoken language in the world. Everybody who wants to get on in life will learn to speak English at some time or another, even the Chinese. So if English is your native language, you already have a huge advantage.

But English is complex, full of illogical structures and spellings, and even great writers will regularly struggle with its grammar. So I recommend you buy a copy of "The Classic Guide to Better Writing" by Rudolf Flesch and A H Lass. Sadly it's not available for Kindle so you'll need to order a paperback, but it'll soon become your best friend. My own copy is dog-eared and marked-up, but it never leaves my desktop!

The biggest complaint you'll hear from professional book reviewers is that *authors don't edit enough.* Sure, you can hire an editor for a few hundred (or a few thousand) dollars or pounds, but until you are selling thousands of books, your primary objective should be to keep your costs to a bare minimum, so you'll need to self-edit (or have a friend do it for you).

There's a huge amount of dross on Amazon, and in the end quality always shines through. So focus on delivering the very best product you can, and the rest will fall into place.

What's New in the Second Edition?

Since the original "Createspace and Kindle Self-Publishing Masterclass" was published in 2013, over five thousand copies have been sold, hundreds of reviews posted, and the book remains a worldwide Amazon best seller.

But although the age-old techniques for writing a book don't change much, the Amazon publishing platform and the book-buying market have made rapid progress in the meantime.

Some things got easier, particularly the technology, and some amazing new software tools have arrived to help independent authors research and execute to a higher standard than ever before. But at the same time the market has become highly competitive, with many more books and authors competing for a share. Quality and speed were never more important.

In this Second Edition, the advice and instruction for working with Amazon, particularly preparing, uploading, and launching your book, has been updated to the current state-of-the art. Amazon now makes it easier than ever for new authors to publish, but it can still take time to figure it all out, and mistakes are easily made. This edition closes the loopholes, and ensures you only do what you need, to get a great result every time.

This year has seen the arrival of three big new Amazon marketing programs: Pre-Order, Kindle Countdown Deals, and the all-you-can-read Kindle Unlimited program. These initiatives have a profound effect on the dynamics of your book's success on Amazon, especially for new authors and first-time self-publishers. If you use them properly, you can earn significantly more money from your books. These programs are fully covered in this new edition.

In addition, the Marketing section has been re-written to take into account the changing social media landscape. I've added a new chapter about building e-mail lists, and how to use them to reach more readers, faster.

I've also expanded the section on outsourcing and freelancers, and included some ideas about co-authoring and working in collaborations.

Finally, the resources section at the end of the book has been updated, and some great new books added to the recommendations.

It's never an easy decision to sit down and update a successful book, because it takes you away from writing something new. But like any other product, you need to keep on top of your maintenance schedule if you want to keep selling copies. Hundreds of reviewers and thousands of readers have been very kind to this book, so it's only fair that I try to provide the most up-to-date and useful information in return.

But it doesn't end there! The Amazon Publishing Platform is an organic beast, and it's evolving all the time as they add new features and programs to enable you to sell more books, so you can increase your Royalties, and Amazon can increase both its profits and its domination of the book business. You need to stay in touch with the changes as they occur, so please take a moment, either now or at the end of the book, to sign up for my monthly Self-Publishing Masterclass Newsletter. Here's the link you need:

http://tiny.cc/wc84gx

If you find something missing, or you have any comments or suggestions, please don't hesitate to e-mail me at

rick@spmasterclass.com

Table of Contents

16 Golden Rules for Successful Amazon Authors

Quality Matters: Whatever you write, and whoever you're writing for, it's important that you never publish anything that attracts criticism on grounds of quality. Edit, edit, then edit again. If you don't, you will get hammered in the Reviews.

Value: You'll often hear from writing gurus that "less is more" in non-fiction. This may work for some people, but it doesn't work for most. Potential buyers can see the number of pages on your Amazon Sales Page, and frankly anything under 100 pages is short-changing the customer unless you're permanently at $0.99, and permanently broke!

De-Personalise: Unless you're a celebrity or you're in a really tiny niche, most readers don't care very much about you, apart from the superficial stuff. This is not your life story, and although anecdotes can serve well in the right context, this is an **information or entertainment vehicle** and you should de-personalise as much as possible.

Write Two Hundred Words Before Breakfast. Some days you just won't feel like you can meet your quota, but two hundred words takes ten minutes or less. If you do this, you'll find it many times easier to come back later in the day and finish what you started.

Get A Great Chair: You'll be sitting in it for anything up to ten or twelve hours a day, so it needs to be the right height, and something that keeps you upright so you're not tempted to slouch back and take your eye off the ball. Success is about productivity, and negating writers' fatigue.

Get A Laptop. It needn't be spanky or new, and it may not be your main writing machine, but you need something portable for those days when you simply can't be at your normal desk. If you have a day job, take your laptop to work and use your breaks or your lunch hour to hit your word count every day.

Don't Worry About Your Title: Whilst writing your book you'll need a working title, but the real thing is a sophisticated and complex beast which does a number of jobs. I can almost guarantee that whatever you choose at the beginning, you'll change it at least once before you get to the end.

Backup your Work Constantly: If you lose a whole manuscript, or even just a chapter, you'll be really pissed off if you have to do it again.

Content is King, but Marketing is King Kong: You need to keep the factory moving, and churn out those great books. But you need to find incremental hours in front of your PC or on your iPhone to keep pushing your messages and building your fan base. You should never go anywhere without an Internet-connected device in your pocket, purse, or handbag.

Hustle: Your book won't sell itself, and neither should you be investing all your royalties in advertising. Be prepared to hustle to get your sales moving. It's really not that tough!

Involve Everyone: If you're just writing a book for some extra pocket money or to feed your vanity, this is irrelevant. But if you're serious about a career as a writer, you'll need to wrap everybody into your new world. You should eat, breathe, and sleep your writing and let the world know that it is your profession and your obsession. Some will turn away, but the majority will give you more support than you ever imagined possible.

Put In More Than You Take Out: Find places where writers like you are congregating, particularly on Facebook and LinkedIn. Help them with their promotions, give them the benefit of your specialised knowledge, but most of all buy and review their books, and you'll find their reciprocation will be amazing.

Never Put Your Picture On The Front Cover: Unless you're extraordinarily good-looking or very well-known. It's a massive turn-off for readers!

Don't Worry If You Can't Think Of What To Write Next: Before this book is finished, the idea for the next one will appear. Just make sure that when it does, you write it down so you don't forget.

Live Your Persona: You're writing a book, so when people ask what you do, tell them you're a Writer or an Author. They will always be interested, and they'll usually be very nice to you. They'll also give you ideas. It's good for your ego, it strengthens your confidence, and it gives you a taste of how it would be if you were doing this full-time.

Stick to the Rules: You can invent a better mousetrap but you can't re-invent the wheel. You will learn to understand the Amazon environment, and everything you need to succeed is in there.

SECTION 1 – WRITING IT

1 - So You Want To Be A Writer?

These days, just about everybody I meet claims that they always wanted to be a writer. So what's stopping them?

For years, being a writer was not the problem. Getting published was! Even if you could write a Blockbuster, or the "How-To" book that the world was waiting for, the process of getting it published and distributed was so hit-and-miss that the vast majority of manuscripts never made it to market.

Then along came Amazon, turning the book retailing market upside down by building their massive online sales portal. They saw that it wouldn't be too long before buying stuff online would become the norm rather than the exception. In what seems like no time at all, Amazon has dominated the Book, CD, and Video retailing landscape, with millions of customers buying billions of units every year.

Once the Internet was established as a viable way to distribute, that is to say that the purchasing procedures and security were in place, the next wave was Digital Media. Apple did it, Netflix did it, and Amazon did it.

Amazon's strength lay in books. In the same way that Apple had combined a highly convenient purchasing system with a sexy device which could store and play music, Amazon's Kindle was set to be the next revolution. Amazon had the book catalogue, and a loyal customer base who were used to buying physical books online and who trusted the Company. Kindle took off like wildfire and now, several generations later, it's synonymous with electronic books. At last count, there were over 30 million *active* Kindle devices in the world.

The big publishing companies were justifiably sceptical in the beginning, and saw Amazon's approach to the market as a land-grab. However as the market matured and the channels stabilised, it became clear that E-Readers would be the future of publishing. Alongside book downloads, the arrival of tablet computers revolutionised the sale of printed and recorded media, and the middle classes of the Western world began to move their media consumption towards an exclusively digital model. Amazon seized the opportunity, realising that consumers who had invested in something like an Apple iPad might not want to carry an additional device for reading books. By launching a Kindle App to run on iPad, iPod, iPhone, and Android smart devices, Amazon ensured that virtually everyone who had a portable screen also had the capability to buy and download books from the Kindle store.

For aspiring authors, the real breakthrough came when Amazon opened up the Kindle platform to User-Generated Content, and the arrival of CreateSpace and KDP quickly transformed the self-publishing market. Before Amazon got involved, "Vanity Publishing," where the author paid for the production and manufacturing of their book, was really the only way to ever see your words in bound-print. Boxes of unsalable publications lay around in cupboards and drawers, often having cost their authors thousands, with little or no chance of ever reaching a public audience. They call it *pulp* in the trade!

Self-Publishing Overview

CreateSpace is a force of nature, probably the ultimate in User-Generated Content. The CreateSpace platform enables any writer with a reasonable competence at word-processing to create a book on any subject, format it, and publish it completely free of charge. Once the manuscript is uploaded to the CreateSpace engine, the book is made available for sale on the Amazon retail website, exactly the same as a JK Rowling or Tom Clancy novel, and competes for sales on level terms. If you, the Author, want one copy, you simply order one and it's printed on-demand and shipped to you, usually within 24 hours. The old term "Vanity Publishing" has now given way to the more accepted "Self-Publishing" and a huge independent literary sector has taken shape. The book business is booming!

Kindle Users Buy More Books

As Amazon's Kindle devices have gained traction, not only have e-books started to take a dominant market share, but also Kindle owners are consuming more titles than ever before. Added to this, the low production-cost of e-books means that Authors are able to make much higher royalty percentages. The sophistication of the KDP Platform has evolved beyond all recognition, and the process of publishing on Kindle is well within the reach of everyone, irrespective of their computer skills level.

As we head in to 2015, both CreateSpace and KDP have reached such a refined level, and the Amazon sales platform has become so innovative, that there is really no obstruction to anyone writing and publishing a book. Thousands of authors now make anything between a small passive income and a full-time living from royalties earned on Amazon book sales. There's no mystery about how to do this, although of course how much money you make will depend on the quality of your product and the success of your marketing. Nevertheless, many people simply don't know where to begin.

There are many hundreds of books on the market about Kindle Publishing, and you may have read a lot of them. I'll recommend some of the better ones later in this book, if you need more technical information as you increase your confidence and ambition. However, the majority of books on the subject make an assumption that you are already accomplished in one or other part of the process, such as Planning and Writing, Designing and Formatting, or Publishing and Marketing. For *this* book, I'll assume that you know nothing about any of these things, simply that you have an idea that you'd like to turn into a book, and an ambition to see if anyone will buy it!

So we'll take a step-by-step approach from the very first spark of how to move your idea from your head to something more tangible, and then the whole process of how to physically create your book and get it to market. You may choose to skip over some of the sections, which is fine, nevertheless I hope you will find some useful information that will answer the "How Do I Do This?" questions that so many new authors ask.

You always wanted to be a writer. Now you can be!

The Amazon Self-Publishing Platform

Amazon's platform consists of three key elements, each of which is a major opportunity for you, the author;

KDP - Kindle Direct Publishing: Amazon's web-based service platform which enables you to upload a complete book to an online server, which then formats it so that it displays properly on Amazon's Kindle devices (Kindle, Paper-White, Kindle Fire) plus the range of third-party Applications which allow Kindle books to be read on Apple and Android devices.

Once the formatting is complete, your book is immediately available on Amazon websites across the world, and you have complete control over pricing and distribution channels. Amazon takes a cut of every sale, and you get 70% (or 35% in some cases).

CreateSpace: This is the physical book Self-Publishing platform. Just like KDP, there's an online dashboard where you upload a formatted manuscript and your cover art. The package is then checked, and once it's approved, the book is made available on the Amazon websites. When someone buys a copy, it's printed on-demand and delivered exactly as Amazon would deliver any other product, usually within 24 hours. The pricing model is highly controllable, and although you can easily make a similar cash amount to a Kindle book, the production cost means that it necessarily sells for a higher price.

Audible: Audible.com is an audio-book publisher that's been around for a few years but which recently became part of the Amazon platform. Audible is similar to KDP and CreateSpace in terms of its marketing functionality through Amazon; however it is for audio books. Audible is so new in terms of self-publishing that I intend to cover it in a future book.

How Easy Is It?

If you can do basic word processing and use a web browser, you can easily publish via CreateSpace and Kindle. Because Amazon wants to maintain consistency of quality across all devices - an important part of their proposition to their millions of customers - they have designed a system which does all the hard work in terms of formatting, so that all you really have to do is write. The upside is that it's simple for the first-time author to get their work published, quickly and easily. The downside is that because it's so easy, it attracts quite a lot of rubbish onto the platform. Amazon do not provide quality control over the material in your book, only the formatting to ensure that it works properly when it's downloaded and displayed.

Like most major search-based online media services, including You Tube and EBay, Amazon relies on a system of User Ratings (Reviews) to self-regulate the quality of the products it sells. The Review system is a critical part of gaining traction when marketing your book, and we'll be examining it in detail in Section 3.

Publishing on CreateSpace is similar to KDP, but here you have more control and responsibility for the final look of your book. It still won't stop rubbish from being published, but it's not particularly discerning in terms of the aesthetic design of your book. If everything you upload falls within the margins (so it will work on the printing machine) you can publish just about anything you want. For the purpose of this book I will assume you have enough self-respect (and hopefully enough ambition to write more than one book) that you're going to take pride in your book's appearance as well as its content.

Luckily, CreateSpace has thought about their authors and realised that not all of them have the skills to be able to format a manuscript in the same way that a publisher might. So they provide a wide range of Page Templates, Cover Creation software, and comprehensive assistance to make your book look good.

It's sometimes hard to believe that all of this is free of charge! But before we get too carried away with how lucky we are, it's useful to understand our position as writers in the food chain, which I would metaphorically summarise like this:

Imagine you're a free-range chicken. You have a nice life, cluck-clucking your way around your paddock, hanging out with all the other happy well-fed free-range chickens, with a nice warm place to sleep and a fence to keep the foxes out. But never forget; your ultimate destiny is to arrive on somebody's dinner table! The whole world of user-generated content (including Amazon, although they are far more benevolent than others I could mention) is about *You as the Product*. The better you understand the ecosystem, the layout of the farmyard, and how to exploit the environment, the more successful you are likely to be.

The Explosion of Online Bookselling and E-Books

The world is full of naysayers who would have you believe that e-books are a passing fad, and even some that say the Internet will never replace mainstream retail. Sure, browsing in a bookshop is one of the few truly free sensory pleasures left in this modern fast-paced world. However, the statistics don't lie.

In 2012, the only book category which outsold e-books was Adult Paperbacks, and then by a very small margin and largely driven by the Fifty-Shades trilogy and its imitators! Amazon's Kindle platform accounts for well over 65% of all e-book sales.

If you spend some time on the online author and publishing forums, you will come across Smashwords, which is the other popular self-publishing e-book channel. Smashwords is an aggregator, which allows you to distribute your book across multiple e-book resellers, and there's no doubt that for some authors it is a viable channel. However, most recent research shows that Smashwords accounts for less than 5% market share in the USA, and although figures for the UK and Europe are difficult to come by, you could reasonably assume that they will not exceed the USA share. There's also Apple's iBooks store, which has around 10-15% market share, but doesn't come close to Amazon in terms of the built-in Marketing opportunities for independent Authors and Publishers, being geared more towards the big publishers and their popular Authors. All of this underlines the necessity to focus your efforts on the Amazon platform.

For non-American authors, it's worth paying serious attention to making sure that your book is suitable for the giant US market. The beauty of electronic distribution is that there are no borders, other than language and culture!

Market forces are multiplied not only by the presence of more e-book titles, along with the convenience and impulse nature of their purchase, but also the massive growth in devices on which to consume them. As if Amazon's Kindle marketing on its own was not enough, every tablet computer and smart phone can download and display e-books. In the education market, the move is towards ubiquitous one-tablet-per-student, so the growth in e-textbook sales is likely to outstrip all other categories over the next few years as tablet prices decline. Larger 12" screen devices are in the pipeline for the schools market. Print revenues are beginning to dwindle as this takes effect. According to some research, digital textbook sales are increasing by over 400% each year, and in one particularly interesting statistic, college students declared that they would be willing to give up sex for a month if they could have all-digital textbooks!

Whilst Amazon's Kindle is far and away the most successful dedicated e-reader in the market, the consumption of e-books is being driven to a greater extent by the take-up of tablet computers. In 2013, the Apple iPad was outstripping the Kindle by some margin, and since then we have seen the arrival of low-cost tablets from Samsung, Google and indeed Amazon themselves with the Kindle Fire.

So what does this all mean for you, the author? Well, the day you upload your first e-book to the Kindle Publishing Platform, you will be entering the fray in a highly competitive market, but one which is currently growing faster, in terms of demand and devices, than any other branch of media delivery. And as we know, a rising tide lifts all boats!

Anecdotally more than a quarter of the Top-100 Kindle book titles on Amazon's platform are self-published, which puts you on a more-or-less level playing field with the "Big Five" publishing houses, who collectively share around 55% of the book publishing industry between them.

As far back as 2011, Amazon's volume sales of e-books overtook physical books for the first time, and by mid-2013 this was by a factor of 15% and rising. Not bad, considering that sales of physical books are also increasing at a huge rate as the whole culture of online impulse-purchase takes hold across the world. Book sales are going up, but e-book sales are going up faster!

And there's more: e-book users typically read 24 books a year, against 15 for conventional book readers. Over sixty percent of e-book consumers pay for their books (as distinct from borrowing them or downloading for free) versus less than fifty percent for conventional book readers.

And if you dare to dream big, try this: Fifty Shades of Grey sold over 250,000 copies as a self-published e-book before a publisher picked it up for print!

So, now that you have a good idea of what Amazon has to offer through KDP and CreateSpace, let's get started on turning you into a published author.

Note: Throughout this nook, you'll come across things that are *allowed* and *not allowed* under Amazon's Terms of Service, which you automatically sign up for when you upload and publish your first book. Amazon, in my experience, plays fair most of the time, and if you follow the guidelines, it's almost impossible to get into trouble. But if you are in any doubt as to what's involved in working with them, you'd be well advised to check the rules for yourself. I take no responsibility for anything that happens to you as a result of following the recommendations in this book, so here's the link to KDP's terms of Service:

https://kdp.amazon.com/terms-and-conditions?ref_=kdp_TAC_FOOT_tac

2 – Both Formats: Make More Money

Right now the scales are finely balanced between sales of paper books and sales of e-books. In fact, more e-books are sold in the major markets than paper books, but of course the value of paper book sales is much greater because of the higher price.

People often comment that they don't see the point in going to the trouble of producing a hard-copy version of their book. It's true that you will probably make more royalty income from e-books on Kindle. However, there are some strong reasons not to ignore the traditional paperback market.

On my first book, I worked with a co-author who didn't like or understand Kindle or e-books, and as a result we wasted at least a year and a few hundred sales by focusing on doing a paperback version from scratch. On the upside, it gave us an extra year to drink lots of wine and dream together about becoming best-selling authors. On the downside, whilst we were working our way through the tortuous formatting and publishing process, we weren't producing anything of value. When I look back, based on the way I work now, I hang my head in shame because I could have written and published at least ten Kindle books in that time.

But I learned a lot in the process. That particular book, though definitely not a best-seller, still moves more paperbacks than e-books. That particular genre (Humorous Travel Stories) seems to lend itself to a physical book, though I have absolutely no idea why! It was only after we had finally given birth to the paperback that I started to get really interested in e-books (which had hardly existed whilst we were writing that book).

Nowadays, I begin each project with the certain knowledge that my book will definitely earn much more money on Kindle downloads, but the physical published paperback, using CreateSpace, is nevertheless an important part of my marketing mix. Here's why:

Not Every Reader Owns an E-Reader, a Kindle, or an Apple device. Amazon would love to reach Kindle saturation, but their traditional book business is alive and well. People still buy a lot of paperbacks, so if you don't publish one you will be missing out on potential sales.

The More Traditional Your Subject, The Higher the Proportion of Paper-Books, because by nature your potential customers are less tech-savvy and less likely to consume books in electronic form. If you want to see an illustration of this, check the reviews on Amazon.com for some best-selling titles which are available in a variety of formats. You can roughly calculate from the reviews the proportion of paperbacks to e-books.

Kids Titles Sell Well Too, I have a series of young people's fiction books in paperback, which regularly outsell their Kindle versions, even though the price is more than double. There could be many reasons for this, but the one I've focused on is the gift market. Kids buy these kinds of books for their friends at Christmas and for Birthdays. So do parents.

Amazon Has Been Around In The USA And Canada For A Lot Longer, having only arrived in the UK, Europe, and Australia more recently. The take-up of digital e-readers as a component of the Amazon customer base in these territories is correspondingly higher, because the Kindle arrived around the same time as the Amazon e-book store. In the USA, the traditional paper book business is still huge, and you will miss out on this if you don't have real books available. Also, not everybody likes e-reading, and won't they tell you so in your reviews if you force them into something they would prefer to have on paper! In the Marketing Section on Reviews you will understand how the disgruntled reviewer can have a disproportionate effect on your success, so you need to equalise before they score.

Review Copies: it's difficult to put your book into the hands of influential readers during your Marketing phase unless you have physical copies. Asking someone to download an e-book, especially of you are not using free promotion, is much less reliable than physically giving them the product. Also, you can make a little extra pocket money with physical books, so if you will be meeting a lot of people whilst you are promoting your book, it's a great idea to have a box of hard copies. It's pretty difficult to sign an e-book!

Your Createspace Manuscript Needs To Be More Carefully Edited And Formatted Than Your Kindle Version (though ideally you should apply the same strict standards to both) because your Kindle book can be revised in a heartbeat, so you'll never end up with a box of pulp. This is why you should never order large volumes of Author Copies until you've put your Paperback live for real, ordered one copy through the conventional channel, and checked it thoroughly. CreateSpace offers the 'Author Proof Copies' service, but this can lose you days or even weeks in transit, especially of you live outside the US, because all Author Copy orders are fulfilled from America.

CreateSpace is free to use, and if you plan your project properly, you will produce everything you need (well mostly) for a successful Kindle publication as a by-product of your CreateSpace project. In many cases it's actually simpler to prepare your CreateSpace manuscript as the main project.

This does a few things:

Firstly, it forces you to pay close attention to your book design and formatting. Kindle can sometimes be unpredictable, and you may have to make some adjustments to your electronic manuscript to get it to display correctly on all devices. However, by doing a physical layout when preparing a CreateSpace paperback version, you get a good look and feel for how you want the end product to appear, and your formatting often throws up idiosyncrasies in titling and spacing which you might miss by going directly to e-book.

Secondly, if you do Kindle first, then go back and do CreateSpace, when you post to Amazon's sales pages the system may not recognise your two products as the same book, and keeps them separate on the site. This is damaging for your sales, because your Reviews for both versions are not combined together. If you complete the CreateSpace manuscript first, there's a facility in the CreateSpace control panel which allows you to publish to Kindle directly from your CreateSpace account. This automatically combines the two titles. If you do it the wrong way round, you may have the added burden of e-mailing Amazon Customer Services to manually combine your titles. This is time and effort you could be using to write your next book!

It's important to your self-esteem and your outward character as a writer that you are able to show physical books to friends and relatives. My wife never really understood what I was doing all day in my home office until copies of my books started arriving from Amazon. As the little pile on the coffee table started to grow, she started to tell people that "my husband is a writer" which is really cool the first time you hear it coming out of someone else's mouth.

CreateSpace is not as daunting as it looks, as you will see in later chapters. I encourage you to consider it as a major component in your self-publishing armoury.

If you are publishing a book purely for so-called 'vanity' purposes, and indeed there are many amateur writers who have no aspiration beyond simply seeing their book in print and ticking it off their bucket list, then you may decide that CreateSpace is enough for you. You write, you upload, you wait a few days, and then you order a few copies. You will pay only for the books you buy (there are no other charges) and you'll pay around the same as if you bought a book from a bookshop. Now that's magic in my book!

If you are planning to publish a technical textbook (for example) to use in a classroom or college environment, then CreateSpace is definitely the way to go. However, you'll probably find that most of your students have Kindles or Tablets, and would vastly prefer it in e-book form.

If you are planning to publish a photo-book, you will undoubtedly find CreateSpace to be simpler than an e-book. You can 'build' an amazing interactive book product for Kindle (Apple's i-Book system is also highly capable and there are some amazing authoring tools out there for this kind of publishing) but that is beyond the scope of this book.

But probably the most compelling reason to go for CreateSpace first is because Amazon's platform will automatically publish your CreateSpace manuscript on Kindle, for no added cost, and usually with no additional work!

3 – Picking Amazon Winners

Non-Fiction

Unless you are an acknowledged expert in a particular field, with unique information which you have either invented or developed, it's a fair bet that most of what you know and most of what is known about any particular subject is out there on the Internet or in libraries, for anyone to discover. This begs the question as to why non-fiction books are so successful, when anyone with enough time and an enquiring mind can probably discover what they need by spending a few hours surfing the web.

The point about short non-fiction books is that people like to have the relevant information collected for them and presented in a sequential fashion. The Internet is a wonderful place, but it is not a panacea. Books (and audio and video presentations) remain in high demand, as a way of packaging the information for easy consumption and repeated reference.

With the sweet spot for Kindle non-fiction books at anywhere between 99c (or 99p) and $3.99 (£2.99), these publications become impulse purchases, rather like smart phone apps. People who are researching a particular subject will often buy more than one book at a time. Indeed, if you are serious about Self-Publishing this may not be the first book that you've read, nor will it be the last!

If it's your intention to write non-fiction, then you may have already chosen your subject. If this is the case, good luck to you and let's get on with writing that book. However, even if you have a book in planning, if you're serious about becoming an author you will need other subjects to write about. Alternately you may not yet have found your chosen subject, and you'll be looking for ways to get ideas.

Obviously the easiest and most effective way to get started as an author is to write about something you know. If you know a lot, that is to say you're an expert in your field, you won't need to do much research in order to put together your outline and your book plan. Alternately you may just be interested in the subject, in which case research is going to play a large part in the creative process.

Research Subjects

It's almost impossible to write an original work on the subject of Self-Publishing for Kindle and CreateSpace, for example. There are dozens if not hundreds of books on the subject, and all of them cover more or less the same information. Different authors will package their material in different ways, maybe targeting a different kind of reader. But nevertheless there is still room in the market for another book on the subject, because the science moves forwards, and new discoveries are made all the time in terms of how to write, market, sell and so on. The same may be said for just about any factual subject.

When I first started writing non-fiction books for Kindle, at least two of the gurus that I was studying used books on "Container and Upright Gardening" as examples, and I was stunned to see the number of titles that compete on that subject. When I wrote my book "How to Master Self-Hypnosis in a Weekend", an Amazon search was returning over 2000 results for Self Hypnosis, but that didn't deter me because I knew that I had a new angle to bring, and a new method to teach. I was right, and my book is high up on the top row of Amazon in the USA and the UK, and has been a consistent best seller for the last twelve months.

The key to non-fiction books is that they must contain information of substance and be useful to the reader. You can't write rubbish or you will be found out by the reviewers.

When you write a non-fiction book, the intention is to give people the information they need either to solve a problem or to educate themselves and encourage them to try something new, such as a sport or a cooking method, or even writing for themselves! When you put your book together you're looking for a new angle to an existing topical subject. The concept of "How-To" is extremely well-established, and it's the opening phrase of a vast number of web searches, so there's a big clue about how to title your book.

There are some great "How-To" books on the market about finding new ideas for non-fiction Kindle books, and a key theme is the suggestion that you should be writing a series of books on similar subjects in order to build a faithful and loyal readership following. This is good advice, however in the short-term, in order to get you started in the writing game, you're just looking for that one killer idea that will motivate you to write it, market it and then spark new ideas for you to move on to the next project. So for now, you should be focusing on something which excites you and about which you can be sufficiently enthusiastic to create 30,000 words.

If you already know the subject that you want to write about, then the first thing to do is check out the competition. Start typing your subject into the Amazon search box, and keep a close eye on the auto-fill titles (so-called *Leading Indicators*) which appear in the drop-down list below. This is the first indication if the subject is well searched-for.

Depending on the territory that you're in, and the browser and device on which you're searching, you may have the option to refine the search results based on various criteria: "new and popular", "price" (low-to-high and high-to-low) "relevance", and so on. Assuming you own a Kindle, or run the Kindle app on your tablet or smart phone (if you don't have any of these devices I seriously suggest you obtain one before you start thinking about writing for Kindle) then a good idea is to select "price: low-to-high". You will see that the first few titles are offered with a price of zero. Elsewhere in this book you will find some information about 'KDP Select', a scheme you can enter, which allows you to promote your book free of charge for a limited period on Amazon. These zero-price books are often on their free-promotion periods, and if you have any sense you'll download them all immediately. Don't be fooled, free books are not poor books, they're just on promotion at that particular moment.

Another reason why books may be priced free, or very low, is because Amazon price-matches against other online book sites. If you want to give away a book permanently, there is a technique for forcing Amazon to zero-price your book, which is covered in the Marketing Section.

Now you have a bunch of books in your Kindle or iPad which you can read quickly, and gauge something about your competition.

"New and popular" is also a good search, because this will show you what's selling. In the Sales Page analysis later on, you'll learn how to get a rough estimate of how well any book is selling by its Ranking. You can also get a good idea of how popular it is (and how good) by looking at its Reviews.

Another great tool, which has nothing to do with Amazon, is the Google Keyword Tool. This used to be a standalone web application, which anyone could access, and which would show you the search volume for a given keyword, along with search volumes for similar keywords in the same category. I guess Google realised that it was providing a free tool which was so well-used that it could now charge for it. So if you now look for the Google Keyword Tool, you won't find it. It's still there, but is now incorporated in Google Adwords, and called Keyword Planner, for which you will need to register an account before you can get to use the tool. You must do this, because it's an invaluable device when you come to title and market your book. At time of writing, there is no obligation to spend money with Google in order to use the Keyword Planner. But you need an account.

If your true aim in writing your first book is simply to be published (so-called "Vanity Publishing") then you may not be too concerned with how saleable it is. However, if like the rest of us you're actually trying make some money out of your literary endeavours, then the less competitive the market you write for, the better your chance of success. If you write a great book on a subject which is highly competitive, and you can get yourself onto the front page of Amazon's rankings, you could make a great deal of money. On the other hand if you can identify a niche which may not be so big, and which has disproportionately less competitive titles in it, you could still do very well, and you will find it easier to get up into the higher rankings for your category.

As mentioned before, when Kindle customers go looking for a subject, many of them will buy more than one book. Therefore it's unnecessary for you to be particularly original, but you need to bring something interesting to the party. The really huge markets are in Health, Wealth and Prosperity, and Love and Relationships. If you want to see what I mean, look for books on Dating. There are thousands of them, but the top few hundred titles sell really well. If you have an angle for a Dating book, and you can come up with a really attractive title, the world will beat a path to your door! Likewise if you know a way that people can lose 5 kg in a week whilst eating chocolate and cream cakes, you may only ever have to write one book before you can afford your own tropical island!

But these are extreme examples, and for the rest of us we're probably going to have to work a little bit harder to get to the top of our trade.

If you already have a subject in mind, one of the best tools on Amazon is the opportunity to "Look Inside" and read the first few pages of all the competitive books in your market. Elsewhere in this book I recommend that you spend a disproportionate amount of time and effort on getting the first 10% of your book as close to perfect as possible, because this "Look Inside" feature is very important when people are browsing for a book to buy.

If the first 10% is excellent, there's no guarantee that the rest of the book will be as good. However if the first 10% is rubbish, it's a fair bet that the rest of the book is just as bad. A couple of hours browsing these 10% extracts will ensure you get a good idea about the quality of your competition.

This is the tool I use the most when judging whether to go ahead and write a book on a particular subject. Don't be discouraged if you find a few really great books; the market is huge. But if you have a few subjects to research, chances are you will discover that at least one of your topics is poorly serviced, and this will provide you with the encouragement you need to make a decision. There's a lot more on the subject of "Look Inside" elsewhere in this book.

Ask yourself; *"Do I have something original to offer?"* You may instinctively know that you can write a better book than anything else on the market on a particular subject, in which case you should get on and write it quickly, then focus all your energy on hustling it up the rankings.

If you are following the pattern of writing a "How-To" book then you will need to be prepared to write a step-by-step guide to how to achieve what you are claiming on the cover. In my experience, people frequently fail at new things they attempt simply because they do not have a system to follow, and if you can lay one out for them (particularly if you can explain briefly what the steps will be in the first 10% of your book) then people will buy.

Logging Your Ideas

In the section about how to get your manuscript written, there's a strong recommendation for a software program called Evernote. When you start to get serious about writing Kindle non-fiction books, you will need to brainstorm ideas all the time. You can jot these down in a notebook, on the back of a cigarette packet, or pretty much anywhere. However, if you embrace Evernote and install it on your phone, tablet, PC, and any other device, you will not only be able to record quick ideas for books as they flip into your head, but you'll be able to develop them as the creative juices start to flow.

Ideas are all around you. You may sit down and start to focus on "what can I write about" but it's more likely that you'll pick up ideas in the course of the day, on a trip to a new place, or just talking to someone in a bar. If you add Evernote on your phone it only takes a moment to tap in the germ of an idea, and it's there, in your face, for development later.

Some people prefer to use the voice recorder function on their phone. This is fine too, but you may find that you make recordings and then never listen to them. If you have an idea after a couple of drinks (which is often when people are at their most creative) then it's entirely possible you'll forget that you made a recording in the first place!

The more ideas you have, no matter how crazy they may sound at the time, the more chance that you'll hit upon a viable subject, or even more than one.

You'll find that once you're in the midst of writing one book, you'll get an idea for the next one with very little effort. You'll also start to refine and reshape your ideas, once you get into the process of publishing your first or second Kindle books. How you will market your book is a huge factor, probably even greater than how you will write it, and until you have experienced this part of the process, your ideas may not appeal to you at first glance.

So, if you have come up with your first idea based on something that you know a lot about, or just a great idea that you found is not well-serviced in the market, you're on your way. If however you are still looking for inspiration, then you'll need to apply some further techniques.

Is there a process that you have recently been through which you found to be complicated? For example; a few years ago I moved from Switzerland to the UK, and in the process I imported a car which I'd originally bought in Switzerland (which is outside the EU) into Britain. Doing this involved going through a series of steps to obtain certification for the vehicle, changing the headlights so that they shine on the other side of the road, having the speedometer and odometer re-calibrated from kilometres to miles, and a whole bunch of other relatively simple tasks, but all of which had to be completed before I could get customs clearance to apply for the registration plates. Sadly, I did this before E-books were popular, but it's a good example of something which I could have written a book about, and which would (in those days) definitely have been a saleable subject.

Travel topics are very popular. Is there somewhere that you've been that surprised or amazed you that you think other people should have the opportunity to explore? You might think that Lonely Planet or Rough Guides have the backpacker tourist market stitched up. But you might be surprised if you look at books for a specific country or city, about how poorly serviced some of them are. Remember, we're trying to write books which will sell in volume at low price. The mainstream tourist guides are normally priced at anything up to $15, and that's much more than just an impulse purchase! I am currently completing a small (20,000 words) tourist book on a particular city through which tens of thousands of people pass every month on their way somewhere else, few of whom ever explore this particular city because there is so little information about it available.

For this book, I will probably price it at 99c in order to build up a following in the travel sector, which is not a subject I've written much about before (apart from my first joint attempt, which really is a turkey; by the way you won't find it under my name, so don't bother looking. We all have to cut our teeth on something!).

This new travel book on its own won't make me a fortune, but if it works I'll then look for a few other cities that I can write about. Remember, there's an awful lot of research material online for just about any place in the world. It helps if you have visited, and it helps even more if you have some local knowledge, but don't let that be an obstacle to you finding out about somewhere and seeing if there's an angle that you can exploit.

Do you have a favourite sport in which you participate, for example golf, or scuba diving, or water-skiing? Is there an aspect of that sport which you think would help others? Take golf for example. There are thousands of books on how to improve your golf swing, and every professional that's ever played in a tournament has written the story of their life, or a particular competition. But a quick look at Amazon will prove that there are very few books aimed at someone who has never played golf before but might like to start. You might think this is a banal subject if you are a golfer, but golf is in the top three participation sports in the world, so there are always thousands of people thinking about learning to play and looking for information that will help them get started.

What I've tried to do here is just give you an overview of the selection process to get you started on writing non-fiction. I would recommend you download and read a book called *"How to Discover Bestselling Non-Fiction E-Book Ideas" by Steve Scott,* which really digs into the research and creativity process, and will give you dozens of techniques and strategies to help you discover your niche.

Remember, at this stage you're just looking for that one big idea that gets you excited and inspires you to sit down and write!

4 – World-Class Writing Productivity

So, you decided on your subject, and you've built your outline, your structure and your plan. So what's the best way to write your masterpiece?

Well, in the end it's going to have to be typed into a computer of some kind. In conventional publishing terms, no editor or publisher is going to be interested in either a hand-written or printed paper manuscript these days, because making changes is far too difficult. As we are mainly concerned with electronic publishing, however you decide the creative process will work for you, in the end your book will be a computer file.

"I Love Typing" is one of those phrases never said by anyone, ever! So for the purpose of this exercise we will simply focus on the best and most efficient ways of using a computer to achieve your desired aims, with the minimum amount of pain and discomfort.

Choosing Software

There are two different methods for writing a manuscript on a computer which dominate the space. Most people will be familiar with a conventional word-processing program such as Microsoft Word, but there are also dedicated author software programs, such as Scrivener, which may work better for you.

Word Processing

Microsoft Word

Microsoft Word is the market leader in WP software. It's been around for years and has evolved in both power and functionality, as computer hardware has become cheaper and more powerful. Apart from its unparalleled capabilities as a text editor, there are thousands of formatting combinations, automated spell-checking, and a host of features which make writing in Word a breeze for both novice and expert alike. If you are familiar with Word there is probably no reason to change, provided you have it on your writing machine. It's my personal weapon of choice.

However, Word lacks any organisational tools to help you with concepts, characters, chapters, or sections. Balancing that out, the Kindle publishing platform accepts electronic manuscripts directly from Word format, and CreateSpace provides physical templates for all its book sizes which integrate directly with Microsoft Word or Open Office. You can also save Word documents as HTML, which can be useful to test your formatting on the Kindle Previewer (more about that later).

The current version of Microsoft Word is available within the Microsoft Office 'Home and Student' package at a very reasonable £109, or the equivalent in US dollars. A more comprehensive Microsoft Office package is available on subscription for around 30% less per year, but for simple writing applications this doesn't make a lot of economic sense.

Note: I recently received an e-mail from a reader who informed me that he felt that I should not be recommending Microsoft Home and Student Version, because its license expressly forbids its use for commercial purposes. I guess he's technically correct, so here's my disclaimer. If you are going to sell books, I recommend you use Microsoft Office 365, which has an annual 'rental' fee, and no such restriction. Never break the terms of a software license. It's illegal.

For me, Microsoft Word does the job very well. If you are familiar with it from your workplace you can't go wrong. However if you are operating on a budget there is simply no need to spend any money with Microsoft, as there are some highly competent word-processing packages available for free.

In mid- 2014, Microsoft released Office for iPad, as a part of the Office 365 program. It's a big leap forward, and increases your options significantly. However it only works well if you commit to storing your documents on Microsoft's OneDrive cloud storage system, which we'll talk about later.

If you want to have document compatibility with your iPad you could also consider an App called iDocs, available from the App Store for around £2.99/$4.25. iDocs loads Word files directly in native format and retains the .doc/.docx formatting so you don't have to do any awkward conversions when you save. You can also use 'Pages' on your iPad, but that will require some conversion each time you load or save a document, making it more suited to those who use Pages on a Mac.

Open Office Writer

If you don't have MS Word at your disposal, and you don't feel like buying it (or renting it through Microsoft 365) you might consider Open Office Writer, which is similar to Word and quite adequate for most manuscript production, and which can be downloaded and installed for free.

Apache Open Office is a highly effective 'open-source' office software package. The word processor is more than you are ever likely to need as an author, and it is fully compatible with Microsoft Office format documents, as well as having an *HTML Save* option which you will find useful for testing in the Kindle Previewer. Open Office is available from a variety of online sources. I would recommend CNet's Download.com as a trusted source.

Google Docs

As a part of its Google Drive service, Google offers a suite of office applications called Google Docs. The word processor, like Open Office, is free to use, though in this case your documents are normally stored online as a part of your Google service. Recently however, Google have made it possible to work on documents whilst off-line, for example when you have no Internet access in a plane or on a train. Later you can integrate your changes back into the online version once connectivity is re-established.

If you are a Google fan, and familiar with the use of their Chrome browser, this may be the program for you. It's free, and it has the added advantage that if you want to work on your manuscript from different machines, for example in an Internet cafe or your work computer, you will be working in a browser window and you can always access your most up-to-date version. This is not available on stand-alone Word Processing programs, although the use of cloud storage such as Dropbox can help, and this will be explained later. Google Docs is the best option if you are using a ChromeBook laptop for your writing, which is a highly effective and very economical device.

Apple Mac Users – "Pages"

Most Apple Mac users will be familiar with Pages, Apple's Word Processing and Page Layout programme which often ships with the machine. If you have a Mac, and you don't have Pages, you can download it from the Apple Store for around $20, which is great value. Everything you need to create a great manuscript is included in Pages, and there's also a compatible mini-version for iPad. Pages documents are also interchangeable with Microsoft Word.

Dedicated Writing Programs

The major drawback of word-processing software is that, although it will often provide an outline function, when it comes to working with multi-faceted subjects in non-fiction, there are very few facilities to assist you with the organisational aspects of your writing.

Keeping your book organized as it gets bigger and bigger becomes increasingly difficult using conventional WP software. So it's not surprising that a number of specific authoring programs have appeared in the market over recent years.

Typical feature sets for dedicated writing programmes include:

- Organising your novel using a project management format.

- Adding chapters to the project at will, and in any location.

- Adding scenes, characters, items and locations.

- Displaying the word count for every file in the project, with target and progress indicators.

- Saving automatic backups at user-specified intervals which allow you to regress back through previous versions if you lose your way.

- Managing multiple scenes within Chapters and allowing easy re-arrangement.

- Viewpoint character, goal, conflict and outcome fields for each scene.

- Storyboard view, a visual layout of your work.

- Drag and drop of chapters, scenes, characters, items and locations.

- Automatic chapter renumbering.

These features are attractive for fiction writers, where keeping track of everything in a non-linear environment can be very demanding.

Scrivener

Probably the most popular authoring program of all is Scrivener. It consists of a text editing tool at its centre, with a huge feature set of organisational tools such as cork-board and index-card tools which enable you to keep control of all aspects of your novel's storyline. For non-fiction, it can be equally useful. If there is a downside, it is that the text editor is not as elegant as a dedicated word-processing application. Nevertheless this is more than balanced out by its organisational capabilities.

Scrivener is available on a free trial basis which allows you 30 days of use. The great advantage is that these 30 days are not necessarily consecutive, so you could indeed complete a fairly substantial project using just the free version. Having tried it, should you decide to progress to the paid version, which is highly recommended, you will pay no more than $50 for the licence.

If you are starting out in the writing game, and you have no particular allegiance to word-processing software, you really should try Scrivener to see if it works for you. But be warned; the learning curve can be significant, to get used to all the different features.

Y-Writer

Y-Writer from Space Jock Software is another dedicated author program which has similar features to Scrivener but presents itself (in my opinion) in a neater and more Windows-friendly manner. Again it enables you to jot down ideas, create scenes, focus on characters and events, and then reorder them as your project progresses. I really like Y-Writer as a tool for the fiction writer because its visual display provides a very elegant method of keeping track of everything that's going on within your storyline. Y-Writer is available in multiple language versions, for Windows and LINUX, and is completely free to download and use.

Other programmes are available, such as Book Writer (www.fastpencil.com) which is directly related to publishing services which you may or may not require. As a novice author, one of the options above should be suitable for you, and you can try them all for free.

Book Writing Software

If you're on any mailing lists, such as JVZoo or Warrior Forum, from time to time you are going to receive e-mails telling you that you really must buy the latest e-book writing software, in order to ensure your books are submitted properly to Amazon.

I recommend you ignore these. There's a thriving little software industry that's grown up by inventing software to deconstruct the e-book process, and actually make it harder! The Kindle and Createspace platforms are so good at recognising and formatting standard file types, particularly .doc and .docx, that there's really no need to mess around with these packages. If you use a basic word processor, just follow the instructions in Section 2, and you should do just fine.

There are some exceptions. KDP provides a collection of free tools for authors who want to publish Children's Books, Comic Books, or convert e-books from another format for Kindle. They also provide a plug-in for Adobe InDesign, if you are using that program (I wish I knew how). You can review and download these useful tools here:

https://kdp.amazon.com/help?topicId=A3IWA2TQYMZ5J6 &ref_=kdp_BS_tool

HTML Editors

If you read other books about Formatting for Kindle, you'll often come across recommendations for Seamonkey, a Mozilla Browser which also doubles as an HTML editor, and Calibre, a third party program which is used as a compilation tool for e-books.

Whilst these are fine programs, and may indeed become useful if you ever decide to move beyond Amazon, there is absolutely no value in using them for Amazon self-publishing, because the KDP and Createspace platforms no longer require you to do any kind of HTML conversion before you publish.

The truth is that there are a lot of out of date books still in the market, which is the main reason for this second edition. If you find any Kindle formatting guide which dates back beyond mid 2014, the technology has already overtaken it so you'll be wasting your time reading about stuff that is no longer necessary!

Other Useful Packages

Whilst the programs above will be more than adequate when it comes to actually writing a book, there are other things you may want to use which will help you with your project.

Dropbox

Cloud Storage is all the rage lately. The idea that you store your documents, in this case your manuscript(s) somewhere else away from your main computer is particularly useful for two main reasons:

Firstly, if you write or edit on more than one PC, you'll need to have the most up to date version available each time you sit down to work. By setting up your folders on Dropbox you won't need to worry about this, as the Dropbox file will be your Master Document, and will seamlessly synchronize with local folders on all your devices, including iPad and iPhone. It's really easy to set up and it works in the background without you having to do anything at all.

Secondly, if you should be so unfortunate as to suffer a hard-drive crash on your home machine or laptop, your documents will be completely safe. Your working manuscripts are your *product*, and they are vital to your craft. Having experienced several crashes at critical moments, I can tell you that the feeling of security you get with Dropbox is priceless.

Dropbox has numerous other uses too. For example, if you want to share files, audio recordings, or videos with the public, you can set these up on Dropbox and simply provide a web-link in your Kindle book, allowing readers to click straight through. I use Dropbox to host Self-Hypnosis Audio Recordings, which can be streamed or downloaded by my readers just by clicking a link. You have total control over security, so even though your files or tracks sit in your personal Dropbox service, they are located in a specific Public folder, so no-one can accidentally or maliciously hack through to your private stuff.

Dropbox is available as a free version with 2GB of storage, and if you need more space and the file-sharing service, you can upgrade to their premium product for less than $10 a month.

Microsoft One Drive

If you are planning to use Microsoft Office applications, particularly Word, on your iPad as well as your desktop or laptop, then OneDrive is the ideal cloud storage solution for you. Your first 15GB is free, and you can upgrade to 100GB or 200GB packages for a few dollars or pounds a month.

OneDrive works in more or less the same way as Dropbox, but it has the clear advantage that Microsoft Office Apps on portable devices can seamlessly access your OneDrive documents online, whereas using Dropbox on an iPad requires a few extra steps to download and upload documents to Dropbox. OneDrive comes bundled with Office 365, Microsoft's software 'rental' plan, which allows you to install Office on up to five computers and your iPad and/or iPhone, giving all of them access to your OneDrive account.

Other Cloud Storage solutions, such as Google Drive and Apple iCloud, work seamlessly for Chrome and Mac users respectively. If you go outside your 'ecosystem' there are dozens to choose from, and there's a survey of the Top 10 here:

http://www.thetop10bestonlinebackup.com/cloud-storage

Evernote www.evernote.com

For research and book planning, I highly recommend Evernote. This is a hugely capable digital version of your notebook, which enables you to gather information, web clippings, notes, photographs, audio clips, and almost anything that might be part of your research, into one extremely well-organized program which can synchronise across computers, tablets and smart phones.

Evernote can appear a little daunting at first and it requires a certain amount of commitment, not least of which is putting away your pen and paper notebook forever! But once you use it for a few days, you'll wonder how you ever lived without it. All the information you gather is available all the time, and if you use Evernote in combination with a word-processing program you will have a very effective organisational tool, which may alleviate the need to use a dedicated author program such as Scrivener.

When you're putting together your book plan, gathering all the pieces of research, storing links to useful web pages (or even the pages themselves), and setting up tasks, checklists, pictures, infographics, and your own ideas, Evernote is there to swallow it all. The App puts everything into Notebooks, which you can organize, and allows you to quickly attach *tags* to everything, which gives you multiple ways to sort and search your material when you need it.

As with almost every software application recommended here, Evernote is available in a free version which is Ad-supported, however the paid Premium version is well worth the investment because of the additional features and extra storage, and comes in at around $50 or £30 per year

If you really like carrying a notebook around with you, there is a specific Moleskine Evernote notebook available, which cleverly integrates with the program, using your smart phone camera.

Evernote also integrates with Live Scribe and Sky smart-pens if you like handwriting your notes in a notebook. These devices wirelessly upload your notes, including audio recordings of any sounds at the time, and store them in Evernote, so that you can easily sort and distribute them later.

Mind Mapping

Since the first edition of this book, I have been exploring Mind Mapping software as an aid to planning and writing books, and it has been a tremendous success.

For some people, the more fluid nature of Mind Mapping works better than trying to aggregate your ideas into a linear outline, such as you might do when planning a book in Word. The Mind Map program allows you switch from idea to idea, and creates an organic view of how you are expanding your ideas, chapters, sections, and even single points.

To get you started, and see if it works for you, there's very capable free software package called Freemind, which is Open Source. If you use a PC, you can download Freemind here:

http://freemind.sourceforge.net/wiki/index.php/Download

There is also a version for Apple Mac, however I have been unable to make it run. There are some 'patches' on the net, but if it doesn't run first time, I generally tend to move on and find something that works. Which brought me to:

SimpleMind

http://www.simpleapps.eu/simplemind/desktop

Simplemind operates in a similar way to Freemind, but it definitely works on a Mac! What's more, there are apps for iPhone, iPad, and Android tablets, and you can seamlessly work on maps on each device, and link them to your cloud store, in my case Dropbox, so that they're seamlessly available on all your devices.

Simplemind has revolutionized my book planning process. From even the tiniest idea, using this tool it's possible to rapidly build the outline of a potential book, as a kind of one-man brainstorm. If you ever worry that your thought processes aren't structured enough, stop. Go get Simplemind and harness the chaos!

There are free versions of Simplemind for trial, but in order to get the full feature set (which is really cool) and synchronize with your mobile devices, you need to invest a little. Simplemind Desktop costs around €24 or $30, and around $6 for the full-function Tablet App.

Writing with Dictation Software

There are several very competent dictation software programs on the market. Using dictation software is a matter of personal taste. On the plus side, if you're the sort of person whose thoughts are well-organized and you have a clear plan, possibly paragraph by paragraph, of your subject material, then you might find that it's quite easy to dictate your draft.

If you really do find typing to be a chore (doesn't everyone?) it's well worth experimenting with dictation software to see if it works for you. There is a danger however that in the rush towards volume you may sacrifice quality. My own experience is that some publications are highly suited to dictation, where long passages of prose are required. Maybe this is why many fiction writers use this system, where telling the story may be ideally suited to verbalisation.

In the early stages of your writing career, it's possible that dictation software could be a false economy. Although it enables you to hit incredible word count targets (ten thousand word days are not unusual for me when I'm dictating) it also necessitates much greater time-investment in editing, both because of the verbose nature of spoken prose, and also because of the lower text integrity qualities when you dictate rather than type. Having said that, if you regularly find that your typing is inaccurate, then dictation may be a zero-sum! Certainly dictation is a lot less tiring.

Probably the best-known commercial dictation software is Dragon Naturally Speaking by Nuance. You can download a trial version, which will allow you five sessions before you need to decide to buy it. The latest version (V13) is extraordinarily sophisticated as it's commonly used by doctors and medical staff, lawyers, engineers and so on, for technical applications.

Unless you already have one, you'll need to invest in a headset microphone. There are dozens on the market starting from about $10. Personally I use a Logitech USB headset, which works perfectly and is very comfortable to wear all day.

Microsoft Windows has speech recognition built-in to recent versions, which also makes a pretty good job of dictating your manuscript. The added advantage is that if you already have Windows, there is no extra cost involved. The disadvantage here is that the Microsoft dictation system does not work well with older versions of Microsoft Word.

The latest Apple Mac computers ship with Dictation, which is initially set up for command and control, and relies on having an internet connection. For serious dictation, you'll need to enable *enhanced dictation* in your System Preferences, and Apple will then download the dictation system to your computer. It's a 500MB file, so be prepared for a wait unless you're on fibre broadband.

I have tested Mac Dictation on a 2014 iMac running Word, and when it works, it's great. Unfortunately, in my case it proved to be unstable, and the online forums were full of people with similar issues, but no clear solutions. If you have an Apple, try it. It's free.

Dictation Software – General Considerations

A few things you need to consider when using dictation software:

If you're writing a non-fiction book, containing lots of technical words or phrases, you'll need to take some time to train your dictation software to recognise these, or it will slow you right down.

If you're writing fiction, and using a lot of names for people and places, you need to do the same thing. The standard vocabulary in dictation software will not recognise unusual names or places, though the common ones should give it no problem whatsoever.

If you're expecting to go much faster using dictation software, on a words-per-minute basis, you may be disappointed. You'll probably be more productive over the course of the whole writing day, because you'll be less fatigued. However don't expect to be able to knock off a novel in a weekend, because good writing is not simply a stream of consciousness.

Dictation software is quite memory and processor-intensive on your computer. If your machine is really old, it may struggle, and even if it isn't you may find the process frustrating whilst you wait for the dictation software to catch up.

Just be very fastidious about your editing if you use dictation software. I recommend you edit every dictated passage as you complete it, before you close it and move on to the next. This may save you a lot of time and frustration in your final editing stage. Sometimes the text you see bears little resemblance to what you dictated, so you need to correct any errors whilst they're fresh in your mind.

One particular scenario that works well for me is when I am writing about a *process*, when I actually want to conduct the process on my main computer, whilst dictating the commentary ("how to do it") into my laptop using Dragon. Using two machines avoids the need to constantly re-engage the dictation software as you switch windows.

In summary, dictation software can be a tremendous asset for a writer. You'll probably find that it isn't suitable for every situation, but if you can get it to work for you it should make your life a little easier, and get you to first draft stage a little quicker.

Summary

For most authors, actually getting the words into the manuscript is the hard part. But by using one or a combination of the methods above, it's possible both to streamline the process and make it easier. Whatever you choose for your first book may not be what you stick with for the long-term, and I would encourage you to try everything. Just remember; Rubbish In, Rubbish Out! No software is going to do the writing for you; that needs to come from you.

Your Writing Environment

If you are already writing, you'll probably have experimented with different situations and environments (home, Starbucks, Pub etc.) and hopefully you'll have found something that works for you. If you're struggling, here are some pointers:

It's All about Productivity

Whether you are writing fiction or non-fiction, aside from Creativity, which is probably environmentally-neutral, the next most important thing is Productivity. In the previous section we talked about using the right equipment and software to make the text input and editing as pain-free as possible, but what about the 'set-up'?

Some people are wedded to their laptops, and write wherever they can find a seat and a flat table. Others prefer to work at a desk, possibly on a full-size keyboard on a PC or Mac. Lately I have been using an iPad with a portable Apple Bluetooth keyboard whenever I want portability. Even the on-screen keyboard on the iPad screen works pretty well if you don't have anything else with you, though constantly editing on-screen with your finger can get a little tedious!

Essentially, you can think and create faster than you can type, so there is no practical limit to how fast you 'want' to type to keep up with your creative brain. So how do you get up to optimum speed?

If you have learned to touch type, maybe as a computer programmer or PA, you have an advantage. If you can look at your screen instead of having to look at the keyboard, then you are very fortunate and your accuracy is probably much better, because you spot and correct your mistakes as you go. For the rest of us, the spell-checker in our WP software is a godsend. When I first tried writing years ago, it was using a conventional typewriter, not even one with an auto-erase feature, and that was truly laborious. Any mistakes had to be corrected using Tippex (another historical curiosity) and it's a wonder that anyone ever got a book finished in those days!

Get a Great Chair

Irrespective of your typing abilities, the most important contributing factor to your word-count productivity, and your ability to stick at it for hours on end, is your body position. Choosing the right chair is critical.

If you have one of those 'executive' style chairs, with the high back, soft seat, and arm-rests, you are potentially disabling yourself in three ways:

Firstly, having arms on your chair is not only an obstruction to free movement, but also encourages you to lean back and stop typing whenever you feel like it. If you look around any office, particularly at secretaries and people who make a living by typing all day, they will rarely have arms on their chairs.

Neither do you want your chair to be too soft, and especially not with a tilt-back option. If you have this recline feature on your chair, lock it out. It serves no purpose in terms of productivity, and any time you tilt backwards you aren't typing, so you're wasting valuable writing time.

But most important of all is the height of your chair. The perfect typing position is when your feet are flat on the floor, your knees form a perfect right-angle so that your thighs are absolutely horizontal, and your forearms are also horizontal, so that you do not have to bend your wrists at awkward angles for your fingers to hit the keys. In this austere position, you are relaxing the optimum muscles and putting the least physical effort into your typing, so you can go on for longer without getting tired or developing carpal-tunnel syndrome, the scourge of typists the world over.

Think of it like this: any sportsman or athlete works really hard on finding the right posture for their activity to give them the maximum performance. Golfers, Sprinters, even Pool or Darts players know what posture will work best when performance matters. You are no different; you are trying to be the best and most productive you can, so good posture is essential.

It can be tricky to find a chair which raises high enough to give you this posture, especially if you're tall like me. But don't give up. Staples has plenty, and they're not expensive. They also have desks in the store, so measure your own work-surface height before you go and try out a few chairs, and you should be able to find the right one for you. Remember, you're looking for high performance if you're going to hit the daily word-counts you'll need to keep your writing factory moving, so don't ignore this; it's really important. If you tire easily and can only manage to bash out a thousand words a day, it'll take you a long time to finish anything worthwhile. With the right posture, and the right mindset and motivation, three to five thousand words a day is not that difficult.

If you like to write at Starbucks, choose a branch where you can replicate this seating position. That's not easy because high-chairs for grown-ups are hard to find, but don't allow yourself to compromise on your seating posture or position even when you're writing out and about, because your productivity will fall and your body will punish you, if not now then certainly in later life!

Smoking?

I know lots of writers who smoke, and I know lots of writers' partners who won't allow them to smoke indoors. And neither will Starbucks! Now I'm a former smoker, who had exactly this issue, and I found that once I started writing full-time I was breaking off every hour or so to go into the kitchen, where I was allowed to smoke, and that meant making a cup of coffee and settling down with the paper. I was losing around a quarter of my daytime productivity, because each time I re-started it would take a few extra minutes to get back up to speed, and I was breaking my flow. Oddly, I was always good at quitting smoking, but I actually enjoyed it when I was writing. It's hard to explain to a non-smoker, but you smokers out there will understand exactly what I mean.

I found the perfect solution, which was to switch to e-cigs (electronic cigarettes). In my book "E-Cig Revolution" you can find out all about this modern smoking phenomenon, and maybe you'll try it for yourself. I started off with simple substitution during my writing periods, and after I while I got so used to 'vaping' that I quit conventional smoking altogether. The result: I'm healthier, more fragrant, a lot richer, and I can happily puff away all day long without stopping what I'm doing, and without any complaints from the family, because the vapour is completely odorless! The by-product of this physiologically harmless nicotine infusion is that my concentration and focus are the best they've ever been. My productivity went through the roof: ten thousand word days are not unusual for me now!

Word Counts: How Much Do I Need To Write?

Writing for a commercial audience requires you to conform as closely as possible to the basic rules and parameters of whichever genre you choose. Amazon readers are quite serious about what they buy, and the Review system enables them to be critics as well as customers. As you will see from our analysis of the Amazon Sales Page, it's really simple for a prospective buyer to see the page count of your book before they decide to purchase it. Even if you're only publishing on Kindle, the Amazon engine makes a pretty good estimation of the number of pages that the book would occupy were there print editions available. In my experience, Amazon usually underestimates a Kindle edition by anything up to 20%, which can work against you if you are at the lower limits of reasonable word-counts acceptable for a particular genre.

At the other end of the scale, writing too much can also be off-putting to potential customers. Striking a balance between the expectation you create with your cover and blurb, versus the number of pages in your book, is really important.

Fiction Word Counts

The lower limit for a viable 'full-size' fiction novel is around 60,000 words, which will equate to approximately 200 pages in a CreateSpace Trade Paperback. Less than this and you risk overvaluing your product at the front-end, and potentially disappointing the reader in the execution. This could play badly for you in Reviews.

Ray Bradbury wrote quite tight: "Fahrenheit 451" was a real lightweight at under 50,000 words, and many of his books are just over 60,000. William Golding's "Lord of the Flies" is just under 60,000, but gets away with it because the content is so incredible and evocative. You should be aiming for more.

Tolstoy's "War and Peace" on the other hand is a real heavyweight, breaking all records at just under 600,000 words. Needless to say this is not a target you should be aiming for. Steinbeck's "East of Eden" weighed in at 225,000 which is more than double what you should be targeting for a first novel. "1984", "To Kill A Mockingbird", "The Unbearable Lightness Of Being", "The Picture Of Dorian Gray", all roll in between 80,000 and 100,000, which seems to be a sweet spot for fiction.

You also need to bear in mind that if you do produce hard copies of the book via CreateSpace, anything under 60,000 words will look like a very slim volume!

Non-Fiction Word Counts

How long is a piece of string? If you're writing a history of the Second World War then it's entirely reasonable that you may want to shoot for 250,000 or 300,000 words. Conversely, a niche "How-To" book may need only 20,000 words to convey all the information that the reader could possibly want. The best advice here is to take a look at a few books in your genre, or similar books to the one you want to write, and check out their length.

Putting yourself in the mind of the reader, how would you value a book? Do you think that a hundred pages is the minimum you should be aiming for? Of course you'll control the pricing for your book, so that needs to be taken into consideration. There's more on pricing later, however if we assume that the sweet-spot for non-fiction is between 2.99 and 3.99 (dollars, pounds or euro's) then it's reasonable to assume that around 25,000 word should be the lower limit.

A typically articulate reader will consume that in around four hours.

The practical considerations when it comes to word count are quite simple:

First; KDP makes a small charge for "delivery" of your book, i.e. they take another small slice of your royalty each time the book is downloaded. You may be aware of Amazon *Whispernet* which is the method by which Amazon is able to offer downloads to certain Kindle devices over the mobile data network free of charge to the user. Of course nothing is truly free in this world, and although Amazon probably have a fantastic deal with the mobile network providers, nevertheless somebody has to pay, and that somebody is you, via the delivery surcharge. This charge is based on file size, and you will soon see it creeping up if you include lots of graphics or diagrams in your manuscript. Likewise the file size increases according to your word count, and if you're targeting one of the sweet-spot price points such as $2.99, a heavy manuscript can take quite a bite out of your royalties.

Next; E-Book (Kindle) readers are more inclined to judge the value of a book by the length of time it takes them to read it, because they often have no other easily-accessible benchmark. Reading on a Kindle or iPad doesn't usually show you conventional page numbers, and although there is a progress bar which gives a good indication of where you are in the book, Kindle customers are smart and they know that the end of the book is often full of acknowledgements and promotional material, so they may be mistrustful of its accuracy.

Finally; CreateSpace costs also increase based on word count, which is entirely logical as they have to print more pages for your book. If you are trying to hit a market-competitive price for a novel, for example, you will need to keep this in mind. There is a Ready-Reckoner on your CreateSpace dashboard which makes it easy to calculate the production cost of your book based on the number of pages and the size. We will examine the CreateSpace dashboard in more detail later on.

How Fast Should I Be Writing?

This is highly subjective, and is largely dependent on how much research and planning you have to do. Some writers assemble their research and have everything they need before they sit down to write the first word. For someone like Malcolm Gladwell ("Tipping Point", "Blink" etc.), who seems to publish a book once every two or three years, you would realistically expect that his research phase is a massive multiple of the actual writing time that he needs. Conversely, for somebody writing romantic fiction, where the vast majority of the material is completely cerebral, the writing and the creativity that goes inside it will probably take up most of the time, though of course you will need plenty of time for cups of tea!

Provided you're well organized, you should have no difficulty in hitting 2,000 words a day. Any less than 1,000 and you'll probably never finish your book, however I myself have had days when 10,000 words have spewed forth, but I'm never quite sure if that's 10,000 quality words!

Organizing Yourself for Maximum Productivity

As with every creative process, writing books has a huge spectrum of methods. Every artist has a different way of approaching and executing the task, taking into account all the variables of a particular book and author relationship.

Broadly speaking, professional Amazon authors seem to fall into one of two main categories. I call them *Super-*

Organizers and *Super-Editors*, and these categories apply in more or less the same way to both fiction and non-fiction authors.

Super-Organizers

These authors spend the most time at the beginning, assembling their research and planning the structure and detail of their book. A Super-Organizer fiction author will probably know how their story begins, progresses and ends, all about the characters and locations, and exactly how to pace their novel.

For the non-fiction author, being a Super-Organizer is about planning, probably down to Section or even Paragraph level, the exact structure of every chapter. The Super-Organizer doesn't start to write until they have a crystal-clear picture. The perfect Super Organizer will never have to think about anything they're missing, because the pre-writing phase ensures that they stay precisely on track, writing to a formula, which they may have evolved over previous book projects. There may be specific word-count targets for each section. The key tool for the Super-Organizer is the Table of Contents or Outline, which is likely to be the first thing they commit to the manuscript, then work tightly, though not necessarily sequentially, to deliver a complete section for each header and sub-header. The Super Organizer takes time at the front end to put everything in place, which saves them a great deal of time and effort at the back-end, the Editing phase. When the Super-Organizer completes the First Draft, they may need only a day or so to complete the editing, focusing on the language rather than the structure. A great tool for the Super-Organizer is a dedicated authoring software programme, such as Scrivener. The key for a Super-Organizer is Discipline.

Super-Editors

The second category, the Super-Editor, works differently. For a novelist Super-Editor, there may only be the vague outline of the story when they sit down to write. These authors instinctively know that if they kick off the first few characters and scenes, the story will construct itself. They're happy to embark on the journey without necessarily knowing the route, or even the destination, and they'll go deep into the creative bubble and write what happens, as it happens.

For non-fiction Super-Editors, they may start with nothing more than a title, or they might have their key messages in mind when they start, and a semblance of knowledge and research to provide a thread, but they'll research on the fly, write out of sequence, and regularly wake up with new ideas and inspiration to add-in features and sections which enhance the project. The outline could be vague, and it may change every day, however over the course of their often-chaotic writing process, the shape will emerge. The non-fiction Super-Editor might thrash out fifty thousand words for a thirty thousand word project, knowing that they can go back once the draft is complete and really build the book from the back-end. A great tool for the Super-Editor is dictation software. Whilst it encourages verbosity, it also ensures that every idea which might make it into the final draft is at least entered into the project, so nothing is forgotten.

The Super-Editor's first draft may be unreadable to anyone else in the world. They will then devote days or even weeks to culling and refining, polishing their work, and forming a logical structure from the disparate parts. The key for the Super-Editor is Creativity.

Many Super-Editors wish that they were Super-Organizers, and some will make the transition over the course of several projects. If you recognise any of these traits in yourself, embrace your style and learn to get the best out of it. No time spent writing or editing is ever wasted.

Outsourcing Your Writing?

Every day my mailbox is full of so-called gurus telling me that every man and his dog can make millions from Kindle books by outsourcing the writing, and how to get a complete book written by a subcontractor or freelancer.

Outsourcing is big business these days. You can get just about anything you want, often to a very high standard, for very little money. You may even have heard that you can get complete books written for a few dollars.

I myself have used outsourced manuscripts for a series of computer-game fan-fiction books. I spotted a profitable niche but realized that I would take too long to research it so that I could write myself, so I went out to the freelance community through ODesk and Elance and found some Creative Writing students who also played the game and enjoyed the books. After checking some samples, I commissioned six manuscripts. Here are some of the issues I faced;

One freelancer, having sent me a great synopsis and regular progress reports, suddenly went radio silent on deadline day, after having requested several extensions. I tried to contact her directly and via the agency but got nothing. She had been paid half the money up front, but I got no manuscript. I have never heard from her, nor found any trace of her existence since.

One story was so difficult to understand that it's still sitting on my laptop until I can find the time to decipher it and sort it out.

- One story was too abrupt, so I had to write another 9000 words to finish it. However, it went on to be the best seller in this genre for me, so I took heart and wrote the sequel myself. That also sells very well.

- The other three manuscripts I commissioned were basically good stories with plenty of context, but the writing quality was sub-standard, and it took me three days each and the cost of a professional editor before I could market them.

On the whole, taken as a block, these books make money each month, but the effort I had to put in to bring them to market was such that the return on investment was marginal for the first few months. For me it was an experiment, and over the life of the project it was probably a zero sum when compared to the opportunity cost if I'd used all that time and energy to write maybe three or four books of my own, which tend to sustain for much longer.

The lesson here is that although outsourcing writing might seem like a good idea, it's not as simple to make money as you might have been led to believe.

Of course if you don't care about quality, you can push the stuff straight out. But if it's poor you will be hammered in the reviews, assuming you ever sell any books in the first place. There is definitely a role for freelance writers, but they have to be carefully managed and your quality control needs to be top class.

It really all depends on whether you want to be a writer or a publisher. I would never say never (that would be hypocritical) but if you're going to outsource manuscripts you'll need to be prepared either to spend a lot of time editing, to bring them up to a good standard, or alternately send them out for editing, which for the depth of work usually required you can expect to spend $300-$750 per book. That's a big financial gamble for most Indies.

However, that's not to say that you should never outsource sections for one of your own books. Sometimes you need a thousand words on a subject which is beyond your own scope, and which will take you too long to research and assimilate.

For example, in the Marketing Section of this book, there's a chapter on Amazon Countdown Deals, which I couldn't write myself because I've never used them. So I asked a friend from my Author 'inner circle', who I knew was experienced in the area, to write it for me. His name is Glen Ford, and he wrote me a first-class explanation, which I barely needed to touch in terms of editing because his writing is so smooth. The deal is simple: Glen gets to include his biography and links to his own books in this book, which is potentially great marketing for him, and he can call on me to return the favor any time in the future. No money changed hands, but both of us got something really useful from the exchange. This happens a lot, and it's a very good reason to cultivate your own 'inner circle' of writers with whom you can establish mutual respect and trust.

Building your Manuscript

If you have used a dedicated Author programme, such as Scrivener, most of the hard work of Building your Manuscript is done for you within the organisational tools. If you have written a linear manuscript, possibly Fiction, a Biography, or a History book, your Chapter order should present no problem.

However, if you have written a non-fiction 'problem solver', such as a *How-To* book, you may find yourself with a lot of disparate documents, probably chapters, which you'll need to organize before you do your final editing and uploading. Here are some useful tips:

- Make sure you understood and used your WP Program's *Headings* functions, using *Heading 1* for Chapters, *Heading 2* for Major Sections, and so on. This will not only stand out on the page when you view your manuscript on screen, but will also enable you to create a Table of Contents automatically.

- Once you have your first draft in some kind of order, create your Table of Contents. Select all the levels of Heading (you can deselect the lower ones later, before you commit your ToC to your finished manuscript) and print it out. You can use it to figure out if everything is in the correct order, and scribble on it as you find errors, or identify things you need to move around.

- Use this Table of Contents to make sure you've have told your 'story' in a logical and sequential way. You can easily go into your manuscript to cut and paste sections in different places, but you need this ToC 'Guide' to give you a helicopter view of your project.

- Focus on *completeness*. It's easy to miss out vital information when you're racing through the first draft, and you need to make sure you plug any gaps before you commit to publication. Of course you can always go back and fix things in a new version, but you run the risk that someone downloads version one and posts a tricky review, which is impossible to get rid of.

Final Editing

Understand that in writing, the word *'final'* is a moving target! But at this stage, you should have assembled your manuscript and you're ready to work through the Editing phase. Personally, I use a mix of self-editing and external editing, depending on the book, and how much time I'm prepared to allocate to it.

Editing costs (and quality) can vary wildly and I recommend everyone try DIY the first time. The objective is to keep your costs down. If you're going to be collecting two bucks a book, the last thing you want to do is to wipe out your first three month's royalties on external services. However, you must be cautious and fastidious. You will turn off your readers if your manuscript is poorly edited.

I read and review a lot of books as part of my Marketing collaborations with other independent authors, and many are deeply flawed. Often, a great idea or story is completely spoiled by the lack of care the author has taken over their grammatical structures and punctuation. Frankly there's no excuse for this. Both Microsoft Word and Open Office Writer have Grammar Checking built into their software, and even if it's not 100% right 100% of the time, a scan of your manuscript is going to point out badly-formed language, and offer you suggestions of how to correct it. It seems that many authors simply run the Spell-Checker (some not even) and leave it at that. Don't do it; you'll be hammered in your Reviews.

If you own a Kindle or an iPad, follow the instructions later in the book to load a copy of your 'finished' manuscript onto your device and do a final read-through just like a customer. You can highlight your text on these devices, so you can then sit down with your manuscript on your PC or Mac, and your highlighted book on your Tablet or Reader screen and do your final tidy-up that way. Alternately you can read it in the Kindle Previewer, but you don't get the highlight feature.

Professional Editors will recommend that you read your manuscript aloud, as a good way to see if the language makes sense, and I would endorse this. There are text-to-speech programs available, such as Ivona, but again these cost money, and if you read aloud to yourself, you'll find and fix most, if not all, of your grammar.

If you are undecided about editing, I recommend you read Karen Crowell's excellent short book "Hiring an Editor" which you can check out on Amazon here:

http://amzn.com/BooGOPWKSU

5 – Perfect Publishing Preparation

Introduction

So, you've finished your writing, and you've edited until your brain is fried! The temptation may be to log into CreateSpace or Kindle and simply upload your masterpiece.

But before you can do that, there are some items you need to prepare. The CreateSpace and Kindle dashboards will be asking you for quite a lot of information, which is essential not only to the formatting and appearance of your book (its quality) but also how it will be searched-for and found, and presented on the Sales Page. Although it is perfectly possible to simply publish, and then go back and make adjustments to this *metadata* afterwards, each change you make will slow down your sales momentum, so the more you get right first time, the quicker your readers will start to consume your book.

Apart from a well-formatted *interior file* (your manuscript), you'll also need to prepare in advance:

- Title and Subtitle

- Keywords and Categories

- Cover Artwork

- How to Receive Your Royalty Payments

- Product Description (your 'Blurb')

Choosing Titles and Keywords

The first thing to understand about Titles and Keywords is this: Amazon is a Search Engine. I'm sure you have at least a basic understanding of what a Search Engine is if you've ever gone looking for something on the Internet. The most popular Search Engine in the world, by a long way, is Google. Some say Google got to be number one because of cool branding, but the truth is that Google's inventors understood human nature a little better than the others, and their early Search Engine soon earned a reputation for giving great results. Although Amazon exists in a different ecosystem to Google, we're going to leverage Google's expertise to help us choose Titles and Keywords, because the sheer scale of their search business means that the 'Wisdom of Crowds' is an invaluable resource for writers.

Amazon is also a Search Engine, but of course Amazon has a vested interest in keeping you inside their ecosystem so that you ultimately buy something. The common factor between Google, Amazon, and the other big Search players is that they refine the results based largely on Relevance. Google makes its money in lots of different ways but does not primarily expect to sell you a product of theirs (though there's a fair chance you'll own some Google products even without really thinking about it). Google uses its omni-presence and expertise to sell advertising.

Amazon drives you down a funnel towards the product you are actually searching for, but also cleverly offers you, at every stage, alternatives and options, which means that if what you were looking for turns out not to be what you really want, Amazon has a safety net of options that may tempt you to veer from your original mission and still buy something whilst you're in their ecosystem. Here endeth the first lesson!

Relevance – The Search Gorilla

Anyone searching on Amazon will generally start out with a fairly clear notion of what they're after. Most people will already have mentally refined their first search input phrase to a sophisticated degree. For example, if you're looking for a book about 'Self Hypnosis' then it's fairly obvious what you'll type into the search box on the first page of Amazon.

In its most basic operational sense, the moment you hit 'Return', the Amazon machine collects all book titles which are set up to respond to 'Self-Hypnosis', and arranges them on the screen for you to browse. The Amazon sales pages' default presentation is *Relevance*. As an author on any subject, you ideally want to be on the first page of results, as near the top as possible, because just like Google, most people rarely browse beyond Page One, and the titles on the first visible screen get the lion's share of the click-through. Irrespective of why they are at the top, human nature assumes that the ones that come up first are the 'best' and the Wisdom of Crowds leads the searcher to automatically assume that up-top is best.

The most Relevant books, and therefore the ones that are at the top of the page, are those which are employing the best SEO (Search Engine Optimisation) techniques. The central pillar to SEO is Relevance (closely followed by Popularity), which is the optimum occurrence of your Keywords in the Title, Subtitle, Product Description and Text of your book.

Of course, depending on the device and screen format that's being used for browsing, there's the option to re-arrange the results by various categories. In terms of achieving Relevance for your book, there are things you can control and things that you can't. So for now, let's concentrate on things that are within your control, then later we'll look at some covert ways to add influence to the apparently uncontrollable factors!

Choosing a Title

Fiction

When it comes to Title Relevance, fiction writers are at a serious disadvantage against non-fiction. Say you have a Gangster novel that you want to promote. It's set in London, and features violent drug dealing gangs and a struggle between good and evil. I happen to have such a novel on my writing calendar, but how do I set up a Title so that its Relevance is going to help me in Amazon Search? Well, people searching for fiction usually have one or two styles or genres that they stick to. For a new fiction writer, it's tricky to break into a genre that's dominated by big names: in this case the Thriller market puts you head to head with people like Lee Child, Tom Clancy, and other giants of the genre. So how precise can you be? Do my target readers search on 'Gangsters', 'London', 'Violent Crime'? Probably not. I can't call it "Drug Dealing Gangsters in London Struggle with the Forces of Good and Evil", though I might use a phrase like that as a header in my Product Description!

The truth is that my title is not going to help me in Search, so I have to look for other ways to get my novel into the line of vision for people searching in my genre. So for this book, what's most important in the short term is to design a fabulous cover, and give it a title which will provoke some kind of emotional response when it appears on screen, however it got there. I want to convey a gritty, snappy, edgy feel, and to make my title and cover look and sound like my genre, just like the other authors I'm competing with. So I called it "Up West". If you have any interest in British Crime Drama, that may ring your bell and motivate you to investigate further. If it doesn't speak to you, then maybe you're not the reader I'm looking for.

If you take a look at Kindle's Top-100, both Paid and Free, you'll see numerous examples of titles and covers that convey a look and feel to the potential buyer, and that's why they're in the Top 100. It's estimated that around a quarter of titles in the Paid-100 category are new, previously unpublished, or self-published authors, which when you consider that all these books are up against the megastar offerings of the Big-5 publishing houses, is pretty good odds.

If you want to see a perfect example of a fiction title which evokes a strong emotional draw, with a cover to match, Gillian Flynn's "Gone Girl" has it all. Even if you're not that interested in the genre (which is left deliberately vague) you almost have to read more. It has sinister undertones, a defined but anonymous victim, it's punchy and edgy, and the simple black cover art really tells you this is a dark, potentially disturbing thriller; exactly the target readership the publisher is seeking.

But nobody is going to go searching for "Gone Girl" in the Amazon search (unless they already saw the advertisements or had the book recommended). However, the intention here is to illustrate how your imaginative approach to titling and cover design can really tug on the emotions of a potential reader once they have arrived at a place where your book is presented as one of their options.

Non-Fiction

Choosing Non-Fiction titles is much more scientific, now that you understand the role of Relevance in the Search Engine mechanism of Amazon.

Your Non-Fiction Title needs to do three jobs:

First it must describe clearly what the book is about. Secondly, it must contain the primary search terms that people are going to use when they go looking for a book on that subject, and third, it must read well and quickly when people scan the page of search results, so as to draw the eye and get them to dwell on your information. Your primary objective, once your book cover appears in a search, is to get people to click on it to learn more. Sorry, but they won't come back later, so you get one shot. Your title and cover must work together and draw people in, so spending time (and even some money) on getting this right is, after the quality for your content, the single most important thing about the process.

If you're interested in finding out more about Cover Design, and even trying it for yourself, please download my free book *"How to Use Stunning Covers to Sell More Books"* here:

http://tiny.cc/a232gx

How Search Works

So let's rewind a little and take a closer look at how the search process works.

Most non-fiction Kindle Books are about how to improve your life in some way or another, or solve a problem, which might range from changing a dripping tap-washer to colonising Mars. As we said earlier, people generally know what they're looking for, and they'll normally enter something highly relevant into the search box, because nobody wants to waste time sifting through thousands of vague results. The most-searched composite phrase usually starts with 'How To' so you could do a lot worse than start your title with that! Other phrases which score highly are 'Learning', 'Beginners Guide To' and so on.

The Importance of Keywords

The essence of Search Relevance lies in "Keywords", which can actually be whole phrases. Search Engines like Amazon's index items according to Keywords, assuming that these are the most likely indicator of relevance to a particular subject. So if you have a book about Self-Hypnosis, clearly the most important keyword is *Self-Hypnosis*, because even a moron can figure out that anyone looking for a book on Self-Hypnosis is going to start with that as the basis of their search. So, 'Self-Hypnosis' needs to be front-and-centre in the Title, and on the Cover Art. And, by the way, so does Self Hypnosis (without the hyphen) because Amazon treats each version as a different Keyword!

But keywords go a lot deeper than just the subject. In a highly competitive category such as Self-Hypnosis (over 1200 results on this search phrase) you'll see that the books that come up on the first page usually have 'Self-Hypnosis' in the Title (or Subtitle – more about that shortly) but a fair percentage of them don't. Some of them aren't even directly about Self-Hypnosis at all, so how are they getting up the rankings?

Amazon's search algorithm (the combination of factors that go to make your book popular or relevant in a search) is a closely guarded secret, and constantly changing, just like Google. However, with Amazon, we sort of know that keywords are really important (alongside sales numbers and average review star ratings). What is harder to pin down is how important keywords are in the different places that they occur. One thing is absolutely certain, and that is that the number of times people search for your book based on a certain keyword, then subsequently buy it, has a strong bearing on your keyword relevance. What is also certain is that, all things being equal, the Keyword in your title outweighs other keyword incidences, so it simply has to be there, for safety.

Your Subtitle

Of course people may arrive at your book with Keywords which are not your number one. In the Self Hypnosis example, similar keywords such as Hypnotism, Hypnotise, Hypnotic etc. will put your book in the Search Results, but they will rank lower, because they are broader (the key here is in 'Hypno'), and they won't get you up to the top if people are searching for 'Self Hypnosis'. However, someone searching on one of these keywords will hit your book if your the specific keyword is entered as one of the seven (five on CreateSpace) hidden keywords that you are invited to enter when you are filling out the information screens prior to uploading your book. You can also use variants of your keywords in your Subtitle, which is weighted highly as well. Expert opinion these days is that the Subtitle is just slightly less relevant than the Main Title, but higher than the 'hidden keywords'. But what about a keyword like 'Trance', which is also a popular search word for fans of hypnosis. If you want to register on these searches, the best thing you can do is to include 'trance' in your subtitle. Remember, these are just simple examples, but I'm sure you get my drift.

There are two other important places where keywords feature, one which is well known, and another which is sometimes regarded as an urban legend, although the circumstantial evidence tends to support the conspiracy theorists. First is in your book's Product Description on its Sales Page, sometimes called your 'Blurb', and we'll look at how to write a good blurb later.

What is clear is that once you put your book up on Amazon, it searches on your Title, Subtitle, and Keywords and in your

Blurb during the process of indexing your book in the Search Engine. Conventional wisdom is that you should mention your main keywords around three or four times each in your blurb, in naturally occurring grammatical language, and this will also help with your relevance to a particular search.

The less proven but nevertheless likely consideration is that your keywords need to be scattered throughout your actual text. There's a demonstration of this shortly. If there are not enough books on a particular subject to fill a complete search screen, because the niche is too narrow, Amazon finds occurrences of your main keyword inside the text of other books which could be virtually irrelevant, and places them on the search screen. It stands to reason that if the search engine is smart enough to find your keyword on page 76 of a book on an entirely different subject, it is quite capable of logging keyword occurrences on your own book that are hidden deep in the text.

In all these aspects, you are looking to tune-up little one-percent advantages in order to rise up the rankings, so even if this is a tiny factor, you should not ignore it. It may turn out to be more important than you think.

So when you browse the non-fiction sections of Amazon, which you should be doing as part of your competitive research, you'll see some quite snappy titles, and some really cumbersome ones too. In the past you might have thought how clumsy they look, but now you should understand that the author is simply trying to cram as many extra keywords (because he's limited to seven elsewhere) into the subtitle, to help with his search rankings. You should be thinking this way too, because your Search Ranking is the single biggest factor in determining the sales success of your book.

Choosing Keywords

When I first started publishing on Kindle, I thought I knew instinctively what would be the most popular keywords for my subjects, but I soon found out the hard way that I was not such an expert. There are two quick and simple ways to see what are the most popular keywords in searches on your subject.

Amazon's Search

Use your primary subject keyword, and type it into the search box (set it up for Kindle Store and/or Books first, because you're not interested in other products). As you type in the phrase, you'll see Amazon start to make suggestions in a drop-down list. Some experts refer to these as Amazon's 'Leading Indicators' and there is a whole science devoted to interpreting them. For this training, I'll keep it simple. Go slowly, and see how these phrases change as you type more of your phrase, and Amazon auto-fills the list. This is showing you popular and recent searches which have been used by people looking for books in the subject category. You can get a good idea of keywords you might use which you now know are in regular use. It's unclear how these keyword phrases are ranked, but let us assume, in the absence of any evidence to the contrary, that popularity and frequency is a major factor. The higher up the list, the more popular the search.

Google Keyword Tool

Not too long ago, there was a free tool on the internet called the 'Google Keyword Tool'. Google being Google probably figured out that people were using this for activities and research that wasn't earning Google any money (such as choosing keywords for an Amazon book), so suddenly in the summer of 2013, the Keyword Tool disappeared, and millions of Amazon authors and assorted internet freeloaders went into temporary mourning. However, it hadn't actually disappeared, but instead had been folded inside the *Google Adwords* environment.

In fact, the tool is even more sophisticated now. It allows you to type in a prospective search key word or phrase, and it will then show you the actual numbers of searches performed on that keyword, which you can sort by numerous criteria such as region, country and so on. It will also show you the figures for related searches. If you use this tool, you can then pick the top five or six by volume, or you can look for more precise terms which are less popular, which may be more relevant to your book but against which you will suffer less competition, which will also help your rankings when you use these terms in Amazon. Remember, these are Google's numbers, so you have to be realistic, but it's reasonable to assume that the split of popularity won't be too different from what going on over the road in Amazon's search engine. And as you'll see in a moment, Google can be a really serious part of your keyword strategy too.

It's a feature-packed device which is too much to explain in detail here, so go and explore the Keyword Planner in Adwords. You'll need to open an Adwords account to get access, but you can do that for free and there's no compunction to actually spend any money once you're in there. Just start by Googling 'Adwords'.

Google Search

By the way, if you get it right, your use of keywords in Amazon titles can give your book a massive leg-up on Google itself. One of Google's primary criteria for ranking a search result is what they call 'Authority'. If you have ever explored Search Engine Optimisation (SEO – A dark art practiced by geeks in caves) you will have heard about Authority. If you have a small business website, you can spend thousands on trying to get up to the front page on Google, but if you don't get Authority into your formula, you'll struggle against bigger competitors.

Well, guess who's the biggest Authority site around? That's right, our good friends Amazon. So if you have a fairly non-competitive key word phrase in your book title on Amazon, if someone performs that search on Google, it's quite likely that your Title (accompanied by a link to Amazon) will pop up on Page One. Try the old chestnut 'Learning Masonic Ritual' again. This is the number one search term keyword for the subject, and my book has it as its main title. Last time I looked, it came up as number three worldwide on Google, and I'm absolutely certain that it's adding to my sales as people click straight through from Google to my Amazon Sales Page. Sure, it's a niche book (which consistently sells hundreds of copies every month), but aren't all non-fiction and self-help titles in a niche of some kind? All I know is that it makes good money, month after month.

Keywords and Search Terms in Your Text

We know that Amazon searches and indexes keywords and search terms from your title, subtitle, and the keywords you select when you upload your book to Amazon's sales portal. But what is less well known is that Amazon also searches for keywords inside the text of your book. If someone enters a search string and there are insufficient books which have the keywords in either title, subtitle or meta tags, it may return titles which have matching keywords somewhere else in the text.

If you want to see an example of this, log onto Amazon.com (All) and enter the search string "Learning Masonic Ritual".

At time of writing, the first two books at the top of the search screen are mine, and it should be clear to you why they come up at the top: because the search string you entered is part of the title of the books. Scrolling down the list you will find two or three other relevant titles which may have been selected on the basis of their keywords as entered in the keywords *metadata* fields during publication.

If you continue down you will find a number of books which appear to have no relevance whatsoever to the search term you entered, but if you expand the results page you should see on the right-hand side some excerpts which contain fragmented versions of the search term.

In some searches, you'll even see *this* book listed, because it has the keyword in the text.

I have not yet found an explanation for this, so I have based my theory only on what I have observed. Different Amazon sites display in different ways on different browsers in different countries, and it seems that if there are insufficient titles to match a particular search string, this deep-search becomes a factor in which books appear on the first page.

If you take this in the context of trying to identify niches and book titles where there is less competition, then you can begin to see how you may also supplement your appearance in Amazon search by including search terms for less competitive niches in the text of your actual book. To illustrate what I mean, if I were to include the phrase "Learning Masonic Ritual" a few times in my "Master Self-Hypnosis" book, I would expect it to show up in this search screen at some point in the future.

Once you know this, the possibilities are endless. Sure, it's not going sell you a million more books, however we are looking for lots of tiny advantages which will get us more exposure on multiple Amazon Search Pages, so this is one worth adding in because it's principally free.

Quick and Dirty Title Building

If you want a quick way to build a tile that contains valid keywords, try this: Choose the three competitive books that you are targeting, and take a screen-shot of their covers, so you can easily recognise them in search screens. Then start entering relevant keywords from your list into the Amazon Search Box. When one of your target books comes up, you'll know that it's probably using one or two of your keywords, so make a note of the most popular ones, and then build your title using these keywords. If it works for them, it should start to work for you.

Micro-Managing Keywords

This book is intended mainly for authors just starting out with Amazon, so I have covered keywords only in as much depth as I believe necessary to get you on the right track. You can spend endless hours refining your keyword strategy, and it may be worthwhile. However, if you feel the need to delve deeper into keyword selection, I recommend you try "Createspace and Kindle Self-Publishing Matrix" by Chris Naish, which outlines a strictly analytical method of optimising your keyword strategy, and actually uses *this* book as it's case study (for which I am highly flattered). You can check it out on Amazon here (the link is repeated at the end of this book):

http://amzn.com/B00KUWR48E

There are also several paid software programs that can help you analyse keyword competition. Amazon allows software developers to plug in to their ranking data, so a dedicated program can search and organize thousands of books at a time, a task which would take you days if you did it manually.

My favourite is AK Elite (www.akelite.com) which costs a whopping $147, but which does a great job.

A cheaper alternative is Kindle Spy (www.kdspy.com) which costs $27. At time of writing, Kindle Spy only runs on Chrome browsers.

Title and Keyword Summary

So now you understand the importance of keywords, and that puts you in the top 10% of self-publishing authors already. Now you have a good idea of how other Amazon self-published authors build and construct titles and subtitles so as to drive up their rankings in the Amazon Search Engine, which is by far the most frequent way that potential buyers will look for books on your subject. Go and mess around inside Amazon's sales pages for a while, particularly in your category, so you can see what other authors are doing.

As of today, there is no known way of viewing the actual keywords (other than the ones we have discussed) that another book is using. If anyone ever discovers a guaranteed way of doing this, I will immediately write you a cheque for four figures!

By the way, some of the so-called 'gurus' of self-publishing will try to convince you that keywords are so well understood and over-used that their effectiveness is rapidly diminishing. Take no notice. They are probably trying to scare you into buying some other form of SEO product or service. Keywords have been the backbone of SEO since the dawn of time, and they're not going away any time soon. The vast majority of self-publishing authors on Amazon don't have a good understanding of how to use keywords effectively, so if you understand their importance, and practice working with them, you are at a huge advantage and you will soon see your books rising in the Search Rankings.

Always remember, copying one person's idea is plagiarism, and that's unethical. But taking leads and inspiration from many sources is called Research, and that's professionalism.

6 – Designing Stunning Covers

If you're planning to publish only on Kindle, you'll just need to provide a front-page cover design. For CreateSpace, you'll need a more complex cover. My recommendation is always to publish in both formats, and if you start by organising your CreateSpace cover design, you can derive your Kindle cover automatically from that during the publishing process. Here we'll discuss the various tools at your disposal, and the following rules which are all important once your book is on the Amazon sales portal.

Your cover is a *Marketing Tool*. If you're writing fiction, the cover will be a key component in the potential readers' impression of what's going on in your book. If you're writing non-fiction, you cover needs to be descriptive, but not necessarily terribly creative. It's very important that your cover can be read and understood in *thumbnail* form, because that is how most Amazon browsers will first encounter your book. The type-size, the colour, and any design artefacts (such as pictures) that you use need to be carefully considered.

When it comes to designing a cover for CreateSpace, you'll need to go a little bit further. This is a real book, and it will need not only a Front Cover, but also a Back Cover and a Spine.

As with the interior of your book, Cover Templates can be downloaded from CreateSpace, either as PNG files which can be used in Photoshop or Publisher, or PDF files which can be used in most other drawing and design programs. If you have some skills in Photoshop or any other graphic design software, you may enjoy Cover Design.

Cover Design Software

There are various ways you can design your covers for CreateSpace. The final target is to upload a print-ready PDF file (Adobe Acrobat) at a minimum of 300 DPI. Most graphics programs will allow you to save their native format in PDF as a final step. Please note that if you are designing for Kindle and CreateSpace in the same session, the Kindle cover needs to be a JPEG. Again, this is a final stage saving process.

Never forget that your cover is purely a device to attract people to your book on Amazon. If you're you going into physical distribution, your considerations might be different, because the whole front, spine, and back of your book will be visible to someone browsing in a bookshop. But for selling on Amazon, only the front cover will be seen.

If you're planning to design your cover yourself, you will need to use some graphic design software. The popular options are as follows;

Photoshop and Photoshop Elements

These are ideal programs for cover design. However, this is not the place to start if you have no experience of graphic design software. Even *Elements*, the cut-down version of Photoshop, is still moderately complex for the novice. If you are experienced with Photoshop, you will get exactly the result you want. The latest version has the ability to add

'Photoshop Actions', plug-in programs that automatically create covers and 3D marketing images. You can also now 'rent' Photoshop via Adobe's Creative Cloud, and there are a ton of instructional 'design a book cover' videos on YouTube.

Microsoft Publisher

My personal preference is Microsoft Publisher, It's a lot simpler to use than Photoshop, and the tools are more familiar to people who use Microsoft Office programs. Using Publisher, you can design your front cover, back cover, and spine separately, then use a CreateSpace Template to insert and adjust them in a single file. Alternately you can load the PDF template into Publisher and work directly in that program. The great thing about Publisher is that it includes Microsoft WordArt, which enables you to do really interesting and attractive things with fonts. If you want to see a DIY cover which works really well, which was created entirely in Publisher, take look at "How to Master Self-Hypnosis in a Weekend". This cover was made using a cropped photograph from Fotolia (www.fotolia.com) as the background, then layering the fonts on top. The photograph cost less than four dollars and is royalty-free!

The downside of Publisher is that it doesn't have a version for Mac. However if you have a newer Apple, you can run Windows programs seamlessly by installing Parallels Desktop or Bootcamp.

Gimp

Both Photoshop and Publisher are commercial programs which have a cost. A free alternative which you can download is called *Gimp*. Gimp is open source, and depending where you obtain it, it may also try to download Adware to your computer. I run a background PC program called Malware Bytes which informs me if any program I download tries to install adware or other malicious software during the installation process, and quarantines it for deletion.

Using Gimp or Photoshop, you can design a cover from scratch if you feel so inclined. Alternately check-out www.coverdesignstudio.com who have a great range of book cover templates for sale. You will typically pay $30 for Kindle only, or $45 for CreateSpace and Kindle. Compared to having someone design your cover (anything from $200 upwards) this route gets you a great cover a really good price, and which you can do very quickly. Their templates give you complete control over all the text items and images. There is a huge library to choose from, including fiction and non-fiction covers.

By using professional templates such as these you will save loads of time, and even a complete novice will end up with a very professional looking cover (provided you don't mess around too much with the format). These templates work well in either Gimp or Photoshop. If you want to see Gimp doing this exact job, there are videos on YouTube.

Amazon's Cover Creator

Both Kindle and CreateSpace have their own online cover design options that are completely free. To take advantage of this you simply click on "Build Your Cover Online" and launch the *Cover Creator*. There are around 25 templates for you to choose from, and the great simplicity of this system is that it automatically enters the title, subtitle and author name of your book into the template. You can then type-in or copy-and-paste your back cover material, your author photo (if desired) and see your complete cover created in a matter of a few moments. The disadvantage is that you will be using a cover which may have been used many times before by other authors. Never mind; you can modify the images and colours to make yours different.

The Cover Creator software is very explanatory and intuitive, and even a beginner will have no problem designing an attractive cover very quickly. Notice that on some PC monitors there is a bug in Cover Creator which appears to cut off the right-hand edge of the front page. Don't be put off by this: simply use your mouse and cursor to slide the cover around in the window and you will be able to see the complete image.

On your back cover, CreateSpace will overprint a panel to contain your ISBN and barcode on the lower right corner. Anything which protrudes into this space will be covered up in the print process. The panel you need to leave blank is 6cm wide by 4cm tall. A quick and simple way to do this, so that text flows around the gap, is to insert a rectangle the same colour as your background (so it's actually invisible), then set it for text to flow around it. Make it 6.5cm by 5cm and everything will look just fine.

Cover Design is an emotive subject. Getting ideas from other books in your genre is a good idea. If you design a good-quality cover, you are levelling the playing field with best-selling authors and big publishing houses on Amazon, so it's really worth thinking it through. It's a good idea to design three or four different ones, then e-mail them out to your trusted friends and ask for their feedback. Be prepared to change your own views, because this is your book and you are highly subjective.

Unless you are drop-dead gorgeous or already famous, try to avoid using your own picture on the cover of your book. Sorry to disillusion you, but really won't do anything for your sales.

Once you have downloaded the appropriate template from CreateSpace, you can open it in your chosen programme. Whichever programs you are using, you can paste the individual elements (front cover, back cover, spine) directly on top of the template, ensuring that you stretch your image to fit exactly the red borderline area. The actual print area is delineated by dotted lines on the template, however if you do not stretch your art beyond these dotted lines to cover the whole of the red border, there is a danger that CreateSpace may reject your cover when you upload it. So bear in mind that what you see at the end will be trimmed very slightly, and make provision for this so that none of your cover art or text elements are too close to the edge, or even overflowing.

In these design programmes, you should leave the Template as a 'Layer' right through to the end of the process. The way to make it visible as you lay images on top is to reduce the *Opacity* or increase the *Transparency* of your images so you can see through them, which helps you to position precisely, especially if you use high magnification (zoom-in) whilst you drag the images around. Alternately you can use 'Bring to Front' on the Template, then reduce the opacity of that layer so that you can still see the guides.

Once you have all the pieces in place, save a second copy of your project. If you need to go back later to make changes or modifications, you'll need the original project with all its separate layers so that you can still work on it. For your final version, you should *simplify* the image or *flatten* it, depending on which program you are using, so that you end up with a single piece of art in a single layer. Before you do this, make sure to restore your pieces to 100% opacity (0% transparency), so that the template is completely invisible (or delete the template layer completely). Once this is done and you have saved it in the native format of your graphics program, you should make a new save file in PDF at the highest quality available (usually called something like 'Commercial Print').

To repeat, your Cover is really important. A good cover will massively enhance sales of your book, and a bad one can bury it. The Amazon Search Results Page is a beauty contest. Look at what's working in your genre, and before you go spending money on commercial covers, have a go yourself at emulating some of the styles you'll see on the best-selling books. You may be surprised at how creative you can be!

However, if you aren't confident that you can get the cover you want using these methods, and you have some money to spend (as little as $5.00 even), here are some alternatives for you to consider;

Fiverr.com www.fiverr.com

If you haven't already come across Fiverr.com, it's a website where thousands of craftsmen and women, from graphic designers to animators to voice over artists, offer their basic service for $5.00. This may sound ridiculously cheap, but the salary for a designer in India, where there are plenty of very skilled creative freelancers, is less than one tenth of that for someone in the US or Western Europe, so that's the equivalent of $50 an hour, which is about the time they will spend on your job. Even South Africa, which has massive creative hubs in both Johannesburg and Cape Town, is less than a third of US or Western European cost.

The good ones turn out great work and they're really quick, because they have to do a lot of jobs to earn a living. However, if you can manage some of the wacky communications issues, and give good clear briefs to your freelancer, you will usually get a decent product. I especially like Fiverr.com when I want some really quick photo shopping done, stuff that would take me an hour or two to figure out. I have one re-toucher who turns a simple job around in ten minutes, which is better than you'd get from your company's internal art department!

There are lots of artists offering book-cover design on Fiverr.com. You could try a few, or alternately you could ask on a couple of Facebook Groups for recommendations, so that you can see real live versions of your potential freelancer's work. As always, it's important to send a tight brief. Make sure your text is unambiguous and accurate, because a foreign designer won't correct your spelling errors. They'll just make your mistakes look nice on the page!

When you brief your designer, it's a good idea to send four or five cover shots, clipped from Amazon, of book covers that you want to take style cues from. You can tell your designer you like a particular color palette, even an image, and of course the layout. A smart designer will do you two or three quick treatments and if you choose one, then it's a good idea to buy another five bucks of their time, which ensures they finish your choice properly and you get an even better job. By using this low-cost system you can even audition several designers on the same project, and you'll have ten or twelve covers to choose from.

Elance and ODesk

Next up are freelancer sites Elance.com and ODesk.com. On these sites, once you register as a client (which is free) and fill in your payment information so that all the agreed transactions are automated, you can post a brief for anything you want. If you load the search keyword 'book cover designer' or 'Kindle cover designer' you will get plenty of responses. In your brief, apart from a description of your book, including the genre, you should request thumbnail samples of their work. Some of them may have websites you can look at, so ask for links.

Shortlist the ones you like, perhaps three, and offer them a 'pitch fee', which is a little freelance contract so you can sample their ideas. Typically a good contractor will want between $5 and $12 an hour, so my recommendation is that you offer them a two-hour fee to produce three ideas in rough. Tell them it's a contest between three designers. This time you may spend around $50 to get back nine ideas from which to choose.

Some people like to put out their shortlist covers on Facebook and hold a beauty contest. I've seen a lot of these posts and they rarely seem to form any consensus; people are all over the place. I guess that's because of the wide diversity amongst your friends, who are usually not the same as the target audience for your book. So how would their opinion really help?

If you don't trust your own judgment, put your favourite three covers on your smartphone, and show them to a few people who (you know) like to read the genre of book you are writing. Just drop it into the conversation when you've had a few drinks to loosen up, and you can expect to get a lot more information about peoples' real likes and dislikes in a real bar than you will in a Facebook comment bar.

When you choose the one you like, award a new contract to the winner to produce your cover. You should order a Kindle version, a CreateSpace version for your paperback, and a 3D version for you to use on things like Facebook posts. You should specifically ask for the following files as the final delivery:

- Kindle cover in the native design format (whichever graphics program the designer used)

- Kindle cover as a high-quality JPG file.

- Createspace Cover in the native design format.

- Createspace Cover as a flattened PDF

- 3D Cover as a PNG file, so you can paste it into promotional material.

These will cover all your bases. You should state in the conditions of your freelance offer that copyright of all materials will be yours once you pay for the job. You need the files because if you decide to make changes in the future, you don't necessarily want to be locked in to one designer.

How much should you offer?

My view on this is that you must balance what the job is *really worth to you* against the quality and attention you want your freelancer to give it. These guys thrive on repeat business, so they'll always try to do the best job they can, but of course the more time you give them, the better the result you'll get back.

My own strategy is to offer them four or maybe five hours work, depending on the complexity of the job. I have heard of people that scalp their freelancers by paying for two hours, but I'd rather have someone who takes care of my work because I'm slightly over-compensating them, than that they rush it because I'm screwing them. People tell me that I am contributing to wage inflation in the emerging markets. You know what, I don't care. Even if the price doubled every three years, it would still be a while before it became uneconomic, and why shouldn't people who contribute to the success of your business be rewarded for their contribution, as you work with them? The extra twenty bucks is nothing to you, given what you are getting for your money. But to a young college student in Ukraine or Bangalore it could buy the textbook he needs for his next exams. There, rant over!

By the way, if you're nervous about running freelancers, don't be! The ODesk and Elance dashboards are very well laid out and really simple to use. Communication with your freelancer is via e-mail, which is all run through the dashboard, so there's no direct contact between you. Your freelancer will file progress reports online if needed, and you can pay for the job either all at the end, or in stages. If you set up the payment stages at the beginning, the dashboard takes care of making the payments on time and charges your account. There's a full range of support services, including complaints procedures.

Crowdsourcing

This is the most exciting option, but also potentially the most expensive. One of the best examples is at 99designs.com, who have handled over 100,000 graphic design projects this way.

Basically, you brief your cover project online, again giving a description of the genre, and maybe the Product Description you're going to use on your Amazon Sales Page, to tell them what the book is about. Your brief then goes out to a fixed number of designers, depending on the package you choose. The cheapest option is £199 and gets you around thirty designers working on your project. You can pay extra for more designers, but frankly you're already going to get 30 almost-finished covers back, and you're bound to like at least one of them. If you can write a brief, it's up to you how much guidance you inject. My recommendation is to take a chance, and let them have the whole idea on their own.

Just a note: you may find that you have to pay your chosen designer extra to produce both your Kindle and your Createspace covers.

Specialist Online Designer

There are many freelance designers on the web who ply their trade based mainly on recommendation. Tracking down a good one is a matter of posting out on your Facebook Author Groups and asking your friends and other members. Everyone is getting covers done somewhere, so you'll get lots of response from a busy group. Most posters will put a link in their post so you'll quickly be able to see the quality of the recommended designer's work portfolio.

Unlike Crowdsourcing, you'll have to stay in touch with the process, because you'll probably be seeing and selecting from rough ideas along the way. Expect to pay $75-$250.

Dedicated Graphic Designer

If you're writing for vanity, or if you have a good graphic designer in the family, this is the ultimate luxury. A cover that is custom designed for you, by someone who gets directly involved at your idea stage. Face to face. You get a broad communications channel to convey your hopes and dreams for your book, and to enthuse the Designer in the process.

Good designers work fast, so a book cover won't take them long in front of the screen. But the time they spend talking to you and showing you ideas, and waiting for your approvals, all has to be paid for. So it's not unusual to run into four figures for a design job if you aren't sure what you want right from the start. For a working author trying to build a business from nothing, a dedicated designer is a luxury you can store away for later, when you're on the New York Times Bestseller List.

Each of these options has an impact on your available time. I do most of my covers myself these days, though I frequently use freelancers to fix photographs, draw specific characters or items, or produce some piece of clip-art that I can't find elsewhere. I often start a book project by designing the first attempt at the cover before I start planning the book. This gives me a title (which often changes later) and a visual representation to work towards. Once I have the cover, I start thinking about the project as a book rather than a job, and that is a good motivator to get on and fill the cover with pages.

SECTION 2 – PUBLISHING

Introduction

Once you have your manuscript complete, your cover designed, and your title and keywords selected, you are ready to start your Publishing Project. Assuming you are following my advice to publish on CreateSpace *and* Kindle, you should do CreateSpace first, because you can then take advantage of the linkage between the two platforms to automatically publish on Kindle using your CreateSpace Project as the starting point. If you are (for some strange reason) not going to publish on CreateSpace, you can miss this section and jump straight to the next one.

7 – Step-By-Step CreateSpace Publishing

In this chapter, we're going to walk you through the process of preparing, uploading, and publishing on CreateSpace. If you follow these instructions, your book should be available for people to buy at Amazon across the world within a few days.

If your book is relatively *standard*, either a fiction format (where the only things which aren't 'normal' text are Chapter Headings), or a simple non-fiction book which doesn't contain a lot of important diagrams or photographs or any subject-specific formatting, such as screen-shots, you will probably want to take advantage of the CreateSpace-to-Kindle automatic publishing conversion, in which case you should do your CreateSpace title first.

The first time you publish on CreateSpace, you should allow at least a full uninterrupted day to get it right. It will get a little bit faster each time you do it. Remember, with Kindle you can go back and change things, and those changes will be reflected in the sales version of your book almost immediately, certainly within a few hours. With CreateSpace, although you can also go back and change things, it's more of an issue, especially if you order a box of author copies to give away or sell, so you need to pay attention to the details and make sure everything is 100% correct before you press the button.

Here is the process, and the things you'll need:

Preparation Checklist

First, you should have completed your Manuscript. You may not yet have formatted it correctly, with titles, chapter headers, pictures and so on, but you need to have completed the actual writing.

Second, the key difference between publishing on CreateSpace and Kindle is this: on CreateSpace you rely entirely on the visual result of your own formatting. You will be uploading a .pdf (Portable Document Format) document, which is 'locked' once it leaves your computer, whereas with Kindle you upload a Word (doc) file or HTML (Hypertext Mark-Up Language) and the Kindle Direct Publishing (KDP) platform and the e-reader device will take care of the major formatting issues. PDF is in effect a 'picture', so the page you send will be the page that is printed, verbatim.

You do have the option to upload a .doc or .docx file to CreateSpace, and let the system do the conversion for you. I would avoid this; the reasons are explained shortly.

So, assuming this is your first time, let's take a look at the steps in the process.

1. Opening your CreateSpace Account

2. Starting a New CreateSpace Project

3. ISBN Options _use CreateSpace_

4. Choose a Book Size and Page Type

5. Formatting Your Manuscript Using Templates _- use my own_

6. Checking and Proofing

1: Setting up Your CreateSpace Account

The first step to publishing on CreateSpace is to create a member account at www.createspace.com. I recommend you use the same e-mail address as your Kindle account, as this makes it simpler for Amazon to marry together not only your titles, but more importantly your royalties, particularly in terms of how they are dealt with by the US tax authorities. Elsewhere in this book there is a section on how to avoid US withholding tax if you are a foreign author, which is important.

Use a memorable password. The first name and last name that you will enter for your CreateSpace member account does not have to be your pen-name, as you will be prompted for this for each title you upload. It really is as simple as filling in this little form, and then you'll be able to log into your account to begin your project.

2: Starting a New CreateSpace Project

Log in to your CreateSpace account and click on *Add New Title* in the left-hand menu column. Enter a name for your project. This can be a working title if you like, because it's easy to change it before you publish. Next choose *Paperback* as the type of project that you want to start and choose *Guided* as the setup process by clicking on *Get Started*.

On the next screen you can amend your project name to be the actual title of your book, and also add a subtitle. Remember what you learned in the section on titles and keywords: with non-fiction books the objective is to try to include important keywords in both the title and subtitle. For fiction, it's unlikely that a subtitle would be appropriate, unless perhaps your novel is part of a series, for example "An Inspector Clouseau Mystery".

Under *Primary Author* you should use the name that will appear on the cover of your book, and you should make sure that it's identical to the author name you're using for the Kindle edition, so that Amazon can marry the titles together later. In the next box you can add *Contributors* if you have worked in collaboration with someone else, and you will see from the drop-down menu that there are lots of options such as *Illustrated by, Introduction by,* and so on. If you do not have a good reason to add contributors, don't look for one. It won't sell more books, unless you got Gerald Scarfe or Banksie to illustrate it!

Next you are asked if your book is part of a *Series*. As this course is aimed at people publishing for the first time, it's unlikely that you will need to enter anything in this box. Later in your writing career you may link some of your books together in a series, which will help to attract buyers and readers to your other work.

Edition Number is useful if you want to keep track of updated versions, which may be useful in some non-fiction genres. Choose the *Language* of your book from the drop-down menu. The final question on this page is the *Publication Date*. If you leave this blank, CreateSpace will assign the date when you approve your book for publication. If you have previously published the same book on Kindle, I recommend you enter the publication date that you used on your Kindle edition. It makes sense to keep everything uniform, and it's conceivable that some buyers will avoid a book with too recent a publication date. If you want to, and if it doesn't interfere with your Kindle publishing, you can enter any date you like here, but remember that you cannot change it later in the process.

3: ISBN Options ◯ ⎸⌄

On the next page you'll be asked to choose an *ISBN* option for your book. You have two choices;

You can click on the first box and CreateSpace will immediately assign an ISBN which will be automatically printed in the back material of your book and on the back cover of the published edition. If you choose this option, your ISBN cannot be used on any other edition of your book, so if you harbour ambitions to move into physical distribution (retail shops etc.) or you are serious about approaching a publisher, you may wish to consider the second option, which is to provide your own ISBN number.

If you are only planning to publish on Amazon, then by all means select the CreateSpace-assigned ISBN option. It's simple and it's instant. If you decide to provide your own ISBN, you will need to go out of the CreateSpace process and approach the ISBN agency for your particular country. Single ISBN's are difficult to obtain, and in most countries the numbers are sold in blocks. For example in the UK, the ISBN agency is Nielsen and then normal processing period is 10 working days. At time of writing you need to fill in a paper form and mail it to them, which is an extraordinarily primitive way of doing things, considering that you are now working in electronic media! Nielsen's smallest block is 10 numbers for which they charge £126. www.nielsen.co.uk

In the USA, ISBN numbers are assigned by Bowker (www.ISBN.org). Bowker will charge you $125 for a single ISBN or $250 for ten in a block.

As you can see, obtaining ISBN's independently of CreateSpace can be an expensive process. But you must ask yourself whether your book has a future beyond CreateSpace and Amazon, because if it doesn't, this is a step you can avoid. If you should sign a publishing deal in the future, your new publisher will take care of all ISBN matters. Bear in mind that author royalties via the conventional publisher route are in the region of 6% to 15% of the cover price. With CreateSpace, you should be earning more than 30% and you will be distributing directly through the world's largest bookshop!

CreateSpace also offers expanded distribution options beyond Amazon and its own E-store, and these do not require you to have independent ISBN numbers. For the purpose of this exercise, let's assume that you've selected the CreateSpace-assigned ISBN and as soon as you press the *continue* button, your ISBN number will be assigned and shown to you on-screen. At this point you should copy the number block from your web browser to a safe place, so you can include it yourself in your manuscript.

What Is an ISBN?

ISBN stands for International Standard Book Number. Each ISBN is a unique numerical identification code and all books published since 1965 have had an ISBN. If you publish your book in different formats, for example paperback, hardcover, or e-book, each variation needs a different ISBN. You will see in the Kindle publishing process that an ISBN is completely optional, and Kindle does not assign ISBN's for E-books. Each country has its own authorised issuer of ISBN's who are free to set their own commercial pricing. If you are outside the USA or the UK, simply Google "ISBN" and the country you're interested in, and you will quickly find your local source.

ISBN formats vary from country to country. Modern ISBN's contained 13 digits, and the first three of these digits refer to the country of issue. The next two refer to the group, the next four are the publisher, the next three are the title, and the final one is a check digit. When your book is printed, the ISBN is also translated into a barcode by CreateSpace. This satisfies the key functions of the ISBN, which is firstly to enable bookshops and distribution channels to identify your book for ordering purposes, and secondly the barcode enables them to manage it within their P.O.S and stock system.

Once you've made a note of your ISBN, click *Continue*. The next stage of the CreateSpace process is all about choosing the size and paper type for your book.

4: Choosing a Size (Trim Size)

CreateSpace offers you a wide variety of sizes to choose from. You should always choose an industry-standard size unless you have peculiar requirements. If you decide to opt for the *Expanded Distribution* option later, your book must be an industry-standard size or it will be ineligible.

Fiction (Trade Paperbacks)

Most fiction paperbacks, once they reach mass distribution, use a *Trade Paperback* size of 11 cm x 17.9 cm (4.375" x 7"). This size is not available on CreateSpace, so it's advisable to select the smallest alternate size which is 5" x 8". For your information, if you use 10 point font size, a 100,000 word novel in this trim size will come in at around 350 pages. Remember, you're in complete control of all these aspects when you publish your fiction book, and it's advisable to spend half an hour in a bookshop looking for a format which you like. It's important to *love* your own book, so that you'll feel good about promoting it once it's published. Choose a format you like, which may require a larger trim size and may use a larger type size. It's really up to you, but don't stray too far away from industry custom and practice. Paperback publishers have been in this business for a long time and they shift millions of units, so there is always a good reason why they choose the design and layout that they do.

For the Interior Type, you should choose *Black-And-White* and for the Paper Colour, *Cream* is the most popular option for novels in paperback.

Non-Fiction

The variation of trim sizes for non-fiction books is huge. The best advice I can give you here is again to spend some time in a bookshop looking at the types of books which are similar to yours. If you have a book with a lot of pictures, for example a history book, you may want to choose a larger trim size which will enable you to display your pictures properly. For the types of books that I usually publish, the Self-Help and How-To genres, one of the most popular sizes is 5.5" x 8.5", and this is the size I use most often. This enables me to publish a 30,000 word book in 11 or 12 point type (which is very easy to read) in around 120 pages, which is an economical option and makes a nice book which can easily be sent out in a padded envelope, and which fits through most mailbox slots.

I have a pet theory that a slightly larger book sticks around because it may not so easily fit into a bookshelf, so it might stay out on a coffee table, or even be passed on to someone else, rather than disappearing into someone's 'library'.

For non-fiction, it's really up to you what colour paper you choose. The trend for modern subjects seems to be white pages, and that is my personal preference.

Manufacturing Cost Calculator

When you have chosen your trim size, you'll see a CreateSpace tool which will estimate your book's manufacturing cost. If you click on this and enter the trim size and number of pages, you'll see the price at which you can order author copies. This is always priced in US dollars, because currently all author copies are printed by CreateSpace in the US. The price per book does not change with quantity (as you would expect, since this is a print-on-demand setup). However if you enter your details into the order shipping calculator, you will notice the massive variations according to your choices. If you are based in the continental USA, you can get copies of your book delivered quickly and at relatively low-cost (although if you want them priority you will pay more than three dollars a book). However if you live outside the US, you're faced with substantial shipping charges to get your books quickly. We'll talk some more about how to obtain author copies at the end of this section, so for now it's simply not an issue.

That completes the first part of your project. If you've filled in all these options, CreateSpace knows what you're planning to do and your project will sit there until you're ready to submit the manuscript (interior file) and your cover artwork.

5: Preparing and Formatting Your Manuscript with Templates

Once you have chosen your book size, you will see that there is an option to download a Microsoft Word template. Word templates also work in Open Office and Apple Pages.

Finish — Formatted Draft Then work it out

CreateSpace offers you the option of either a *blank template* or a *formatted template*. If you are publishing for the first time, particularly fiction, the formatted template is a very useful tool. It chooses the popular Garamond 11 point font and sets up Chapter Headers, Page Numbers, and Page Headers, as well as showing you where to insert all your front material such as Title and Author Name, Copyright Information, Dedications and Contents. If you have completed your fiction manuscript, I recommend you select this formatted template, which will save you a lot of time.

If your book is of the non-fiction variety, and contains things like Subheadings, Section Titles, Numbered Lists, Bullet Points, Indents, Diagrams or Pictures, then the formatted template will probably frustrate you. The formatting is so tight that once you start inserting things which are not considered to be *body text*, you can very soon have a messy project on your hands. It's almost impossible to move Chapter Headers around, and this formatted template does not lend itself to the creation of an effective Table of Contents, which is essential in a non-fiction book. For non-fiction I recommend you use the *blank template*, which simply sets up the Word or Open Office document with margins. In the case of both these templates, the gutter offsets (for left and right-hand pages) are perfectly setup to ensure that your printed book will look professional and slick. With the non-formatted template you can choose your own fonts and type size, just as you would if you were preparing your manuscript from scratch.

Compiling from a Dedicated Writing Program

If you have completed your manuscript in a dedicated writing program such as Scrivener, you will need to use the *Compile* function to export it to your Word Processor before you can upload it to CreateSpace. Remember, in this phase of the project you're acting as a book designer, and it's important that you're able to disregard the content and focus on the format, so that it will look nice when it's printed.

Choosing a Design Format

Whereas plagiarism is a crime against humanity, when it comes to book design, imitation is the sincerest form of flattery, and also the most reliable method! As you are now an Author, I'm sure you have cupboards full of books, so you can choose one that you like and use it as a design template for your own book.

In the self-publishing industry, there's a great deal of advocacy for employing external services such as editing and design. This is to be expected, as many writers also make a living from these additional services, including yours truly!

www.ricksmithbooks.com

For me, although design is extremely important, I believe that the objective of the novice or beginner Self-Publisher is to keep the costs as low as possible. If you are producing a novel, the interior design is a piece of cake. As previously described, you can easily emulate the standard design of a trade paperback just by looking at a few, and identifying the key points which are: Margins and Spacing (taken care of by the template downloaded from CreateSpace), choice of Font and Point Size, and the front material such as Copyright and Titles, which is simply replicated from any published work.

If your book is a heavily-formatted non-fiction work, there may be a case for you hiring an external designer. However, be aware that you'll encounter a range of prices from as low as a couple of hundred pounds or dollars right up to several thousand. In my humble opinion, anyone who has made it this far and is ready to self-publish a book has enough creativity to do the work themselves. We'd all like to publish *beautiful* books, but for the sake of this initial exercise, *adequate* is probably good enough.

If you spend a little time online, you will discover that there are more people writing about writing then there are actually writing books! It's very easy to get caught up amongst the debates over what constitutes good design and what you should and should not do. Try and do it yourself, and if you really find that you're failing and you can't find anyone to help you for free, only then should you consider looking outside for professional assistance. Both Microsoft Word and Open Office Writer have all the editing and design tools you need, so maybe you just need to spend a little time getting familiar with those programs so that you can use them effectively.

Working with the Template

Download the template you're going to use, and it will open in your word processor. If you are using the formatted template, I suggest you open up two windows on your screen with the template on the left and your manuscript on the right. It's then a simple matter to copy and paste your text into the template, overwriting the existing text.

If you run out of chapters in the template you can simply copy and paste to add more.

If you have already uploaded the same manuscript to Kindle, try not to change anything. It's very important to maintain consistency across all formats, especially in the first 10% of your book (the *Look Inside* portion).

Justification

Here's my rule: all books should be right-justified, that is to say that the text should be aligned on the right-hand margin so that it forms a neat rectangle is when viewed on the printed page. When you prepare a Kindle manuscript it's unnecessary, because the KDP system handles that. But now that you're designing the printed page yourself, you need to take care of this particular formatting detail.

Other formatting details which will not carry across particularly well from a Kindle manuscript (if that's your original copy) are things like paragraph spacing, titling, and some numbered lists and bullet points. So once you've pasted your manuscript into the template, you will need to spend some time working on the overall look and feel. I find this one of the most enjoyable aspects of self-publishing, as it offers you the opportunity to add beauty and creativity to your words, particularly in the non-fiction genres.

If you're working with the formatted template, you may find that the stock font is Garamond or Book Antiqua 12 point, which are very attractive fonts and perfectly readable. However they are not particularly economic. If you're concerned about the cost of production of your book, you may want to play around with some other fonts to see if you can get the page count down a little. As an example try Cambria, and you could see your page-count reduced by more than ten percent.

Troubleshooting Createspace Templates?

CreateSpace templates can occasionally exhibit some issues. One particular problem that may occur is that when you paste the copied text from your original manuscript into the template, particularly if you do it in one large block, some of the page size formatting seems to get lost. Maybe part of the document reverts to A4 size (the Word default document size). This appears to be a Microsoft problem in some software versions.

By trial and error, the most elegant solution I have discovered is to save a new version of your original manuscript as a .txt file, which removes most of the formatting, then copy and paste the text into the template. Of course, that means that you will then have to work your way through the formatted manuscript and insert formatting from scratch, but in terms of time spent this is more efficient than wasting a day trying to figure out where you've gone wrong!

Another alternative is to open a copy of the original manuscript in Open Office, then copy and paste the text from there into the Word template in Microsoft Word. I have no idea why, but this also solves the problem of pages reformatting their sizes. Again there is some reformatting of text and headers to be done, but it's relatively minor in the scheme of things.

6: Checking and Proofing

Now you have all your material in the right-sized template, it's time to make sure that your layout and design conforms to market expectations.

Design Considerations: Fiction Manuscripts

As mentioned earlier, it is better to follow a convention for fiction, which is modelled on what the big publishers do when they put out a trade paperback.

Title Page

The first page is a right-hand page and should simply show the book Title and the Author name. If the title is short, you should use block capitals in a simple font, something more than 18 point size.

Front Material

The next left-hand page should contain all your *Front Material*. Depending on the amount you intend to include, you may use a very small point size (six point or even four point) as no one reads this information except lawyers, and why would you want to make things easier for them!

Acknowledgements

Page 3 (the next right-hand page) is for your acknowledgements. If you publish a Kindle book, it's possible to have the Front Material and Acknowledgements pages, and in fact any other superfluous material "behind" the starting page, so that when the reader starts to read the book, they by-pass this information completely. However, when you publish a physical book, it's likely that the reader will start from the very beginning; hence your Acknowledgements page may indeed be read. Keep it brief. Once you are a bestselling novelist with a huge recurring publishing deal, that's the time you can thank your entire family and everyone else for all the help and support they've given you.

For this, your first book, it's just about ego! If you want to thank people for having given you help and support during the writing process, it's much nicer to give them a signed copy of your book once it's published. Thanking some random acquaintance who gave you "faith and encouragement that kept up your enthusiasm during your bleakest days" is so self-indulgent that it could indeed turn off a reader picking up your novel for the first time. Trust me; most people don't really care why you wrote the book or how you felt about it. A novel is about escapism and entertainment, and it is rarely necessary to establish your credentials or real-life experience for writing it in advance.

Let the quality of the writing and the story stand alone. You can connect with your audience later.

Blank Pages

[handwritten: RT HAND]

If your acknowledgements finish on a right-hand page, you should then insert a blank left-hand page and start your story on the next available right-hand page. Creative writing courses may tell you that the use of "Introduction" or "Prologue" is a useful tool for the novelist. It's up to you, but there will be a percentage of your readers who may not comprehend that an introduction or prologue is actually an important part of the plot, and they may actually miss it out and go directly to Chapter One. So unless you have a compelling reason to break convention, the first part of your creative writing content should be Chapter One.

[handwritten: ALSO RT HAND]

Chapter Headings

For Chapter Headings, just use a number! You do not need to include the word "Chapter" nor do you need any flashy underlines, text boxes, or artwork. Books are like Marmite (Vegemite). Any feature you insert which breaks from convention will undoubtedly impress part of your readership, but it may turn off others. For that reason I would recommend you use "plain-vanilla" design and formatting. If the worst crime you commit is to underwhelm people with the design of your book whilst entertaining and enthralling them with your creativity and storytelling, that's just fine.

Your text must be right justified throughout.

Indentation

In conventional fiction book design, the first line of each chapter is usually not indented. Subsequent paragraphs are indented, and there is no extra line space between paragraphs. Lines of dialogue are indented exactly the same as paragraphs. You can set up these parameters in your WP tools, usually under *Paragraph>Indentation*.

Page Numbers

Each chapter begins on a new (usually right-hand) page. Page numbers are always at the bottom of the page and central. You should use a standard footer from the menu in your word processor to insert page numbers automatically. Just make sure that you observe the minimum printing margins which CreateSpace demands. If you get this wrong don't worry, because CreateSpace will check your pages before committing to print and let you know if you need to make any adjustments.

Choosing Fonts

We mentioned your choice of Font earlier in the section. If you're using Microsoft Word or Open Office for your final design, you have a choice of hundreds of different fonts. You would be well advised to stick with the font which came with the downloaded CreateSpace template or one of the really popular fonts, notwithstanding the requirements to potentially reduce the number of pages. You should never reduce your font size lower than 10 for the body of your book, and 12 point is probably too large. If you have followed the advice about replicating a bestseller, then you may be wise to print out a few test pages to see how your font reads. Your fallback position should be Georgia 11 point. On no account should you ever use a sans-serif font such as Arial or Calibri for a work of fiction. These types of fonts are harder to read in large blocks of text and should be avoided.

Hyphenation

Because you're using right-justification, you should set up Automatic Hyphenation in your Page Layout menu. There are numerous other hyphenation options in your WP software, however by simply using automatic hyphenation you should get a satisfactory result and avoid any messy line formats.

Dialogue

Dialogue convention these days uses a 'single quotation mark' rather than the more grammatically familiar "double quotation mark". Remember, question marks and exclamation marks are always contained within the quotes, as is all punctuation related to the speech itself. If you have any doubts about how to format speech within your novel, you can quickly check a couple of paperbacks from your own library to see how other authors and publishers do it. You may find some variation from title to title, so choose one that you like and that looks good, and simply replicate the formatting. Creative Writing courses spend months trying to explain all the nuances of dialogue formatting. However there are very few major rules and you can easily learn them by reading someone else's book.

Sections and Headers

If, for whatever reason, you are breaking your book into sections or parts, you should insert a blank page with the words (for example) "Section 2" to separate the parts.

If you want to use page headers, you should put the author name on the left page and the book title on the right page. You can find the facility to do this in your "headers" menu in your WP program.

It's advisable to make each new Chapter begin on a right hand page, though this is not obligatory.

The Back End

At the end of your story, you should leave at least one blank page. After that you might insert some more information about yourself, other books you have written, and even an extract from your next or previous novel. This is really useful, as many readers come off the end of your story and are thrust into an anti-climax. It's an opportunity for you to fill that gap and drive them towards another book of yours, or some method of keeping in touch with you, for example a link to your website or a short biography (if you can write an interesting one).

Design Considerations: Non-Fiction Manuscripts

In my opinion, the design aspects are not only more *important* for a non-fiction book, but also allow you to inject some *creativity* into the process. First of all, you may be using diagrams, illustrations or even photographs in a non-fiction book. It's important that you understand how to insert these and manipulate them for best effect in your WP program.

Image Manipulation

Any images you use should be a minimum 300 dpi. You can use JPEG, GIF or BMP images, which can be easily inserted into blocks of text using the *Insert Picture* button on your WP toolbar. If you use GIF's the file size will be smaller, which may help with your Kindle version.

When you insert an image into a text block, you can use the *Format Picture* control (easily accessed by right clicking on the image) to adjust the Layout. If you select *Tight* you will see your text flow around the image and you can then drag the image around the page to reposition it in the most attractive place. If you want to use the full page-width for your image, try to position it so that it breaks the text in a logical manner. If your image is less than the full page width, then you should make sure that the text which runs around one or both borders is broad enough to read properly. Make sure that you keep the image within the margin guidelines for the page.

Experiment with image positioning, you can't do any damage. If you find that you have got yourself into a mess, simply use the *undo* controls to step back until you have got yourself out of trouble again. Remember, when it comes to inserting images in the CreateSpace environment, what you see is what you get.

The treatment of images and pictures is *completely* different in a paperback than in a Kindle format.

Tables

If you are using tables, you may have converted them to image files for your Kindle version. It is possible to use (for example) JPEG images of tables in the same way that you would use any other photograph or image in your CreateSpace manuscript, however I would recommend that you re-do any tables in the native WP format. This is a little bit of extra work for you, but the end result will look much neater and you will be able to edit the tables, which you cannot easily do with a JPEG.

So, starting from the situation where you have copied and pasted your entire manuscript into the appropriate template, formatting your non-fiction manuscript requires the application of a little more design than in the previous example, the novel.

Title Page

Your title page can contain more information. It is likely that a non-fiction book will have a more elaborate title and probably a subtitle, and these should be included, as well as the author's name, any qualifications or letters after your name, and possibly a shortlist of any other relevant books that you have written, perhaps in the format: "also available..."

Front Material

The first left-hand page should contain the relevant front-material, such as disclaimers, copyright statements etc. This should occupy no more than one page.

Acknowledgements

If you are including dedications or acknowledgements, these should be placed on the next right-hand page. Whereas a lengthy acknowledgements section is self-indulgent in the fictional world, especially for a first time novelist, a non-fiction author may include prestigious acknowledgements to further establish their credibility or expertise in the subject material. See what other authors in your genre have done, and replicate the ones you like. Just remember that this is a print book and it could hang around for many years, so you should choose your acknowledgements carefully.

Table of Contents

Next comes your Table of Contents. Your WP program has the facility to make an automatic Table of Contents, and if you explore the features of this function you will see that you can adjust the levels to make the Table of Contents more or less detailed. If you already prepared your original Kindle manuscript, you should have used the WP software's Titles,

Headers etc., to designate the levels. Play around with the automatic Table of Contents function and you will see that it will automatically pick up all headings that you previously inserted in your manuscript. You can limit this to only "*Heading One*" for example if all you want to list are the chapters, or you can expand through *Heading Two, Three, Four* etc if you want to place every subject in your Table Of Contents.

Just remember: an important part of the sales tools on Amazon is the "Look Inside" feature, and this is no different for a print book. If your Table of Contents is too long and elaborate, you will be taking up a lot of this real-estate. Depending on the subject matter, this may be a positive thing, as it will allow potential buyers to see the huge range of subjects that you have covered in your book. Alternately, you may want to limit your Table of Contents to just chapter titles, and use the rest of this early portion to give people a flavour of your writing.

Preface

If you are including a Preface, you should always start it on a right-hand page. The Preface is ideally an overview of the *reason* for your book, and also because of the "*Look Inside*" function, it forms an integral part of your marketing material. A good way to begin writing your Preface is to take the blurb that you have prepared for the Amazon sales portal and either repeat it verbatim, or adapt it. I find that a bullet-point list of the key features of your book is useful in the Preface. We'll look at blurb in more detail in the Marketing Section.

About the Author

At the end of the Preface you may decide to include a section called "*About the Author*" to further establish your credibility to write on the subject. Many people find it difficult to write about themselves, and the rule of thumb here is that "less is more". Nobody is really interested in what you ate for breakfast or that you particularly like hanging out in Irish pubs with women of loose reputation, but they would probably like to know if you have a Master's Degree in Philosophy or are a world leader in Zeppelin Building. One tactic which I have seen used to good effect is to put a very short introduction about yourself at the beginning of the book, and then a longer biography at the back.

How to Use This Book

The next section that you may choose to include is "*How to Use This Book*". Once again, remembering this forms part of the "*Look Inside*" portion, you should aim to give the reader a short instruction course on the best way to work through your book. Some types of non-fiction books need to be read in chapter order, whereas others may be more like a reference-book format. Whatever the case it's always a good idea to explain to the reader how you would ideally like them to read the book.

From a marketing perspective, it's useful to include details such as your website address, and any other contact details that you want the reader to have. I also like to try to establish a little rapport with the reader, so I usually add a "signature" at the end of all this front material. Something like: *Rick Smith, London, December 2012.*

White Space

If your book is of the "Self-Help" or "How To" genre then you really need to concentrate on making it easy to read, and for people to be able to find relevant sections quickly. The rule here is to use lots of white space. Sure, it's going to add pages to your book, but it will make the whole experience more satisfactory for the reader.

Every paragraph which contains relevant information should have some kind of header or title.

Unlike fiction, you should leave a blank line between each paragraph. My preference is not to use paragraph indentation, as the blank line does the same job. Neat formatting in terms of paragraphs and justification will make the whole page look visually appealing.

Sub Headings

When composing titles and headers, it's a good tactic to frame them as a question. Imagine that every header and title will appear in the Table of Contents (even if it won't) and how that will speak to a potential reader. Try to frame headers as questions which the reader might ask themselves, and you will be gaining subconscious agreement from the very start.

Numbers and Bullet Lists

You can use numbered lists or bullet points to great effect in a non-fiction context. Your WP program will automatically format these for you, and unlike Kindle you know that *what you see is what you get*. Again, if you're concerned about how to format these for the best reading experience, consult some similar books and simply replicate their formatting.

Chapter Numbers

Whereas in the fiction arena, Chapters were simple numbers, in non-fiction you may want to be a little more creative. You can use icons, underlines, text boxes; just about anything you like to make your headings more attractive and appealing.

Don't overdo it, because what really matters is the information contained in the text and images.

Emphasis

Use *italics* or **bold type** for emphasis; try to avoid underlining.

Use extra line spacing (whitespace) to break up sections. Always start Chapters on a new right-handpage. Use *Insert Page Break* to make sure this formatting stays in place as you run through the various stages of your editing process.

As with all creative writing, avoid the over-use of exclamation marks and commas. You'll go back and do a ruthless cull of unnecessary punctuation before you finally publish your manuscript.

Grammatical Integrity

If you are at all worried about your English grammar, or any other aspect of formatting in your writing or your manuscript, it's a good idea to use "beta-readers" to give your book the once-over before you commit it to print. You may have the most wonderful content, but if it is badly formatted and grammatically incorrect this is likely to show up in your Reviews later on, once your book starts selling. In the Marketing section we'll be discussing the importance of Reviews in getting your book ranked and also enticing buyers, so if you're nervous at all, don't hesitate to use people whose abilities you respect to do a critique.

Page Headers and Footers

Inserting *Page Headers* is a useful way of designating Chapters and Sections in non-fiction books. If you use your WP software's *Section Break* functionality, you can insert a different Header for each Section or Chapter. By placing the

Chapter name or the Section name in the Header, it makes it easier for people to flip backwards and forwards through your book when searching for a particular subject.

You should only use the *Page Footer* for page numbers, which should be centred in the same way as in the Fiction section above.

Screen Display Issues

One of the disadvantages of CreateSpace templates in Microsoft Word when used to prepare a print book manuscript is that it's impossible to display the pages on the screen in the same way that they will appear in your book. Because your manuscript will always start with a right-hand page, you cannot insert a blank left-hand page at the beginning. Consequently when you put two pages side-by-side on the screen you will always be looking at a left-hand page on the right and a right-hand page on the left. I have not yet found a way to overcome this, so it's something you just have to get used to. This is only a matter of how the margins appear. When I am preparing a manuscript for CreateSpace, I find myself zooming in and out all the time. By reducing the magnification and looking at lots of pages on the screen at once, you can get a really good feel for how your text flows through the book.

Splitting Paragraphs

There's a lot of debate in self-publishing circles, and book design in general, about splitting paragraphs, so-called *widows* and *orphans*, and keeping lines together. Your WP program enables you to control this precisely. The best way to do this is to select all the text (Ctrl+a), right click *Paragraph*, select *Line and Page Breaks*, and adjust each of the pagination options individually. Personally, I turn them all off and then go through the manuscript and set my page breaks manually for the printed version. In some cases if you allow your WP software to automate the process, you will end up with many more pages and lots more blank space in your book then you really need. Remember, the objective is to make your book easy to read, not to win a prize for design.

After you have done your first pass through your manuscript and fixed all the major issues, you will probably need to go through two or three more times and clean up the detail. On these final passes, it's important that you are looking at the pages as a whole, rather than reading your book again. As before, zoom out so you can see ten or twelve pages at a time and you will very clearly observe the patterns. You'll be surprised at how easy it is to spot things that still require adjustment.

Spell-Checking

When you think you've done everything, run your Spell-Checker. With all the manipulation you been doing on the manuscript over the past few hours, things may have slipped. Your spelling and grammar check will pick up any badly formed sentences, especially if you have included unnecessary commas or spaces. This is your last opportunity to pick up any little inconsistencies.

While using your Spell-Checker, you may have used English spellings for words. If you are a British author and you want to sell books in the USA, you should consider modifying spellings of words such as *memorise* and *colour* into the American style. Anecdotally, American readers find English spelling a little disorienting, whereas English readers are so used to the vast library of American literature that they don't even notice American-English spelling. Your decision may have a lot to do with the context of your book, however remember that the American market for Amazon is more than five-times the size of the British market.

Saving and Naming Your Files

Once you have completed the editing, proof-reading, and formatting of your manuscript, save it carefully with a unique file name to ensure that you don't get it mixed up with previous versions. My preference at this point is to delete all previous versions, but if you feel the need to keep these, create a folder called 'Previous Versions' and park all the old stuff in there.

I use the following naming convention for manuscript files, so that I can always find the most recent one first time:

- Date, in the format YYMMDD, so it will sort numerically

- Book Title (as an acronym) such as 'SPM' – Self Publishing Masterclass

- Format; either KDP (Kindle) or CS (Createspace)

- MS (for Manuscript)

- Version Number: vX.X

So the current file for this book is called:

140925 SPM CS MS v1.1

If I use a version as a published file, by uploading it to KDP or CreateSpace, I save it as a new version with the next version number, and 'UL' tagged on the end.

7: Uploading to CreateSpace

CreateSpace offers you the option to upload your manuscript in various file formats, including PDF and .doc/.docx. My preference is to use PDF, generated on my own computer, because that way I control the formatting. If you upload a formatted .doc or .docx word file, you may find that Createspace slightly alters the formatting, and if the position of your page breaks is important to you, this might disrupt your layout. This is less of a problem for fiction.

Once your manuscript is to your own satisfaction, upload it using the *Browse* button. The CreateSpace conversion and review process takes less than 5 minutes for a text book, and once it is completed it will offer you the option to review your book by selecting the *Online Reviewer*.

Dealing with Proof Issues

You may also see a message telling you that you have a number of manuscript *Issues*. Usually, these issues refer to items in your manuscript that are overflowing the printable area, or graphics that are too low-resolution. Once you open the Online Reviewer you can clearly see how your book will be displayed in print form, and you can scroll through page by page. Any issues will be clearly redlined so that you can inspect them and make the necessary corrections in your original manuscript. The best way to do this is to open your WP manuscript in a window alongside the Online Reviewer and make your corrections dynamically as you find them.

Hopefully you completed all your proofreading before you uploaded the file, in which case you will be flicking through page by page and simply looking (admiring) the design and layout of how your book is going to look in print. However, if you have time and you feel inclined to do so, you can read your entire-book from cover to cover in the Online Reviewer, and this will simulate how a customer will read it when you finally print it. Once you have decided what to do about any overspill, and if you've spotted any typography mistakes or things you want to change, you should go back to your original WP file and make the changes there. Then save the file again with an updated version number, make a new PDF, and upload it once more to CreateSpace. Repeat the online review process until you're happy that it's as good as you want it to be. For many new authors, this review process is very exciting because it's the first time they see their manuscript in book format.

Once you're happy that you have an acceptable version of the manuscript uploaded to CreateSpace, you can put away the interior of your book and move onto the next stage, which is uploading your Cover.

There is no necessity to complete all the stages in the CreateSpace process in one sitting. The system will remember what you did, and each time you come back to it you will see on your CreateSpace dashboard exactly where you are in the process. Nothing is ever lost!

Uploading Your Cover

Assuming you already completed the production of your cover, you're now ready to upload it by selecting *Upload a Print Ready PDF Cover* and browsing for the appropriate file.

The upper limit for file size is 40MB. If your file is too big you'll get a warning message and you won't be allowed to enter it into the text box. If this happens, you need to go back to your graphics program and resolve it there. What tends to happen with Photoshop is that if you flatten the file as a .PSD (Photoshop's native format) file and then save again to PDF, the file size expands massively and may exceed the 40 MB limit. The solution to this is to save the .PSD file as a JPEG, at a medium (level 8) quality and select *'JPEG compression'* and *'medium quality'* when you make the save. This will dramatically reduce the file size and you should now have no problem in getting the CreateSpace system to accept your upload.

It's unlikely that you'll experience any problems if you design your cover in Publisher. In this case you save the native .PUB file directly to .PDF.

Once you've entered the correct file name in the box, click *Save and Continue* and wait for the upload to take place, which will take a few minutes.

Finalising Your Title

Once CreateSpace has accepted your cover artwork, you will see a summary page which gives you the opportunity to check the basic information about your Title and Subtitle and make editing changes if you need to. Remember when we entered the Project Title at the beginning? We said that you could use a *working title* and that you would have the opportunity to modify it later. Now is your chance. Make sure that your title and your subtitle (if applicable) agree 100% with what you have written on the cover of your book and in the front material, because if there is any significant variance, Amazon will not accept your book onto its sales portal.

Also shown is your ISBN, and it is worth keeping a note of this elsewhere. The trim size is summarised and the number of pages, and the file name of the interior manuscript you uploaded before. If you want to upload a new version of your manuscript, you can do this by hitting the *edit* button. The final box states the file name of the cover art-work PDF you have just uploaded, and again if you are having second thoughts, the time to make changes is now. Simply hit the *edit* button and you can pause the process, revise anything you need, and upload a new version.

If you're happy that everything is in order, you can now submit your entire package for review by CreateSpace by hitting *Submit Files for Review* at the bottom of the page.

Next you will be informed that your files are being checked, and you now have the opportunity to select your Distribution.

Selecting Distribution

By using the CreateSpace process you are automatically selected to sell on Amazon.com, Amazon Europe (which includes sites for all the major European countries) and the CreateSpace e-Store. Further down the page you will see a box for *Expanded Distribution*. For the purpose of this book, we will ignore expanded distribution, which is a large subject all of its own. That's not to say that you can't select it, but you will need to investigate all the implications and royalties for yourself. The margin (royalty) on Expanded Distribution is dramatically lower than Amazon sales, and it may adversely affect your ability to hit a realistic price point for your paperback. Expanded distribution is a $25 additional option.

Press *Save and Continue*

8: Setting Your Prices

The next page you will see is the *Pricing* page. Here you have the opportunity to set pricing for the US, UK, and European Amazon websites. Based on the price you choose, this page will calculate and inform you of the royalty you can expect to receive. You can play around on this page for as long as you want: until you hit *Save and Continue* your prices will not be registered on the system. If you have in mind an amount of royalties that you believe you should earn, you can constantly adjust the prices until you see the figures that suit your ambitions.

If you're planning on running a promotion to try to kick-start sales of your book, then it may be worth selecting the lowest possible price initially, in order to make a book more accessible. We'll discuss this in more detail in the Marketing chapter. Remember, you can go back and change the pricing on your book any time you like, and it will take effect within a few hours.

Assuming you have not stated any pricing on your cover (don't ever do this), CreateSpace will not print any pricing information on there either. So you have complete freedom and flexibility to chop and change your pricing at will.

Calculating Your Royalties

If you have written a book for an international audience, start by entering a suitable US dollar price and see what it does to your royalties. You will see that the royalty you can expect from the CreateSpace e-Store is significantly higher than that which Amazon.com will pay you. Bear in mind that very few book buyers will search directly on the CreateSpace e-Store, though if you are running marketing links from your website you may want to drive purchasers there directly. In reality, the vast majority of your sales will be through Amazon, so that's the royalty you should focus on.

Below these two options you will see the calculated royalty for expanded distribution, irrespective of whether you have selected it. If you play with the USD pricing you will see that you need to raise it quite high before you can see a decent royalty from expanded distribution. This is a good illustration about how royalties work in the real publishing world. As we said at the beginning, you can earn a lot more through Amazon and Self-Publishing that you than you ever will by going to a conventional publisher, unless you write a blockbuster! For this reason, I generally ignore expanded distribution. There is a school of thought that says if your book is very successful via Self-Publishing, a conventional publisher will ultimately come looking for you, and then it will be taken out of your hands. In the meanwhile, concentrate on Amazon.com and the other Amazon sites as the place where the bulk of your sales income is likely to come from.

Pricing is covered in more detail in the Marketing section of this book. In order to have total flexibility of your pricing, you will need to un-tick the boxes which are intended to automatically calculate and collate pricing across the UK and European channels, based on the US dollar price. In my experience, Amazon Europe is almost an irrelevance if you are publishing in English language. One guideline you might choose to operate is to try to align your royalties more or less with what you are receiving from Kindle sales, because as you will see from the section on Sales Tracking in the Marketing chapter, it makes the calculation a lot easier on a week-by-week and month-by-month basis.

Aligning your book prices with books in your genre or category is a good idea. Unlike Kindle, where you can promote at very low prices by selecting a 35% royalty for a period of time, or even for nothing if you enrol in KDP Select, you cannot price your CreateSpace book below the minimum list price which is shown on the screen.

9: Reviewing Your Print-Ready Book File

Within 24 hours, you will receive an e-mail from CreateSpace telling you that your proof is *Ready to Order*. This means that CreateSpace is nearly ready to print your book. Go into your CreateSpace dashboard, which should launch at the point where you have uploaded your file. You have a choice of ordering a printed hard-copy for proofing, which is fine if you have plenty of time on your hands, but the best alternative is to launch the Online Reviewer and check the file on your PC screen.

Checking the Whole Package

The first time you used the Online Reviewer, you were only able to look at the interior of the book. Now, the cover has been included and you can look at it in its cropped format. At this point, you need to check carefully, because it's entirely possible that some of the elements which you used when building your cover may have moved on the page, relative to the cropping. A common issue here is that your front or back cover art is off-centre, and this needs to be corrected.

If you have made any small errors, particularly with respect to the Spine position, Createspace will usually correct this, and whilst that's useful, it can throw some of the other elements out of whack, so take care over your cover review.

Last Chance Edits

You can modify and upload a new cover file as often as you want before you go to press. If you have any issues with the cover, now is the time to fix them and then save the new file as a PDF ready for uploading.

The dashboard gives you options to edit three items

1. Your Title and Subtitle

2. Upload a Revised Interior Manuscript file

3. Edit and Upload your Cover.

Once you have made any final adjustments to your cover art you can browse and inserts the new file name (I suggest you *do* give it a new file name) and it will upload as before. You must now wait for the proofing process to happen again, which will be advised to you by another e-mail once it is ready.

To activate the proofing process, assuming that you have made changes, click on *Submit Files for Review* and a box will open telling you that your files are being checked. Click on *Continue* and you will pass through the Distribution Options screen for a second time and arrive at the Pricing screen again. You should not need to make any changes here, so click on *Save and Continue* which will then take you through the *Description* and *Additional Information* screen again, until finally you arrive at the *How It Works* screen. Now you wait.

Whilst you are in this *proofing* stage, don't be afraid to repeat the process and clear up even the smallest errors that you notice. It may have taken you many months to write your book, and each time you recycle the proofing process it will be less than 24 hours before you can see your new version, so it's worth it. If you have plenty of time on your hands, you may choose to select *Order a Printed Proof*. If you are based in North America, this is quick and cheap. If you are based elsewhere in the world, the shipping delay may frustrate you. However, if you are at all nervous that you do not fully understand what you are seeing on the screen when you view the Digital Proof, take the time.

Ordering Proof Copies?

Ordering physical proof copies, ordering author copies, and the alternative, which is to order from your local Amazon site, is a question of balancing the cost and time against your specific needs. Being a UK-based author, I rarely use either of the first two options because the shipping times and cost make the whole thing marginal, versus simply ordering copies as I need them from Amazon once it's published. As every book is different, and every author is in a different location, you will need to work this out for yourself. The only way to accurately see the cost of printed proofs, of which you can order a maximum of five at this stage, is to go through the ordering process from the *Proof Your Book* screen. Don't worry, you can cancel the process before you get to actually confirm the order, but in the meanwhile you can see the cost of shipping and the price of the books themselves. When you have the information you need, you simply go *back* in your browser until you get to the beginning.

Final Approval

When you are absolutely certain that your book is the way you want it to look, you can then approve your proof by clicking on the *Approve* button and then confirming your approval. The next dialogue box will show you when you can expect to see your book appearing for sale.

Obtaining Author Copies

If you are in North America, you may now order copies directly from the CreateSpace e-Store. You will recall that when we set up the pricing, your royalty amount on CreateSpace's own store is higher than on Amazon. For US authors, ordering copies from CreateSpace is probably the cheapest way to obtain them for yourself. And it's quick.

The fundamental problem with proof copies and author copies is that for some reason best known to CreateSpace, these are only printed in the USA. Once your book appears on Amazon.com and Amazon Europe, the commercial copies will be printed locally to where they are required. For example, I can order copies of my own books on amazon.co.uk up to around 4pm on any day and they will arrive at my home the following day. To me, this is a truly amazing service. And it pretty much underlines why, unless a major publisher comes in with a great offer, there's really no other way that you could achieve such a convenient and economical service for publishing your books.

It generally takes around five days for your book to come up on the Amazon sales sites. It won't necessarily appear on all of them at the same time, and I have known my books to come up on Amazon.com within three or four days of proof approval.

10: Automatic Kindle Publishing

Once this is completed, there's nothing more for you to do but wait until your book appears for sale on Amazon. However, if you have chosen to do your CreateSpace manuscript first, it's now possible to automatically publish an identical version on Kindle. This screen will appear automatically, and to take advantage of it just click on the big blue button which says *I Want to Publish My Book on Kindle*.

KDP Quick Dashboard

Rights and Protection

Confirm that you have the necessary publishing rights. You will then be asked to select DRM (Digital Rights Management). If you choose not to enable DRM for your book, you run the risk that it may be pirated and distributed free without your knowledge. Even though you are technically covered by Copyright, the chances of you ever stopping this are next to nothing. If, however, you enable DRM, it should not impede any promotional activities you undertake. Kindle users will still be able to lend the book and gift the book.

Here again, there are two schools of thought. If you enable DRM (which is permanent) you will invoke a certain amount of protection, but it's far from fool proof. I regularly find pirate PDF copies of my books available on (mainly Russian and Chinese) free download sites. Without a big publishing house behind you, with their army of lawyers, there's not much you can do to prevent this, so it's best to ignore it. DRM will not stop this.

The alternative is to leave DRM disabled. In this case, your book may find its way to a few more pirate sites.

In a previous life, I spent many years working with content-protection in the TV business. Millions of dollars are spent by the studios in closing the pirate loopholes, largely in the mistaken belief that if you prevent people from getting hold of stuff for free, they'll start paying for it. This is nonsense; they'll either find a different place to get the content, or simply download other content that isn't protected. You might reasonably take the view that anyone who reads your work, however they obtained it, is a potential customer for more of your books in the future.

After I published the first edition of this book, I received an e-mail from a reader who was very vocal on the subject of registering your copyright. As I am a strict believer in the 80-20 way of working, I choose not to do so. I cannot envision any situation in which I would ever have the personal resources to enforce any breach, so I'm comfortable ignoring it. However, this is a matter of personal choice. But I did promise I would include it in this edition.

The rules on copyright are set according to the Berne Convention, and you can check the international signatories at the World Intellectual Property Organization (WIPO: great acronym) here:

http://www.wipo.int/members/en/

Each country has it's own registration authority. In the USA, you can register your book at the US copyright office. Other countries have similar systems, and rather than list them here, I recommend Google as your starting point!

Whether or not you choose to go through the registration process, you should always include a copyright statement in the front matter of your book. Here's a copy and paste paragraph you can use:

> "© 2015, [your name]. Except as provided by the Copyright Act [date, etc.] no part of this publication may be reproduced, stored in a retrieval system or transmitted in any form or by any means without the prior written permission of the publisher."

In any case, once you publish you have legal proof of the date of your publication, which should be sufficient as evidence should you ever find yourself caught up in a copyright dispute.

Submit Your File

Click on *Submit My Files to KDP* and you will be transferred to the Kindle Direct Publishing site where your bookshelf may already be set up (if this is not your first encounter with Kindle). KDP will then import your interior and cover files from CreateSpace, which will take a few minutes. Once this process is complete your book will appear on your KDP Bookshelf with *Action Required*. Click on your title.

Preview Your Kindle Book

Scroll down to item 6: *Preview Your Book* and launch the online Previewer. You can now scroll through your book and see exactly how it will look on a Kindle Fire device.

You can change the Device that you're viewing, including Apple devices such as the iPhone and iPad. We'll look in detail at the various KDP Preview options in the Kindle section in the next chapter.

At this point, the processes are the same as if you are publishing directly to the KDP platform.

CreateSpace Summary

That's it for CreateSpace. You're now a Published Author. As soon as your book appears on Amazon, you must order a copy. Of all the things that will happen to you during your writing and self-publishing adventure, there is nothing quite like the thrill of opening the Amazon parcel and seeing your first book, in your own hands!

But avoid the urge to order lots of copies, because if there's anything wrong you'll be stuck with them. I often find that I want to change the cover fairly soon after first publication, and if you're stuck with dozens of the old ones, you'll have wasted your money.

Next, we're going to walk through the Kindle publishing process. If you've used the automatic Kindle publishing function, a lot of this may be irrelevant to you. However, if you're unhappy with the way the process has altered or formatted your book when you look at it in KDP, you'll have the chance to rework and upload a new version of either your manuscript or cover, and all of this is covered in the next Chapter.

8 – Step-By-Step Kindle Publishing

Introduction

In this chapter we're going to walk step-by-step through the processes to publish your finished manuscript for Kindle, for which we will do the bulk of the formatting in a word-processing program.

In the first edition, I explained that the key steps to get up on Kindle involved converting your WP file to HTML, a one step process and which is handled within your WP program. If you are familiar with HTML, you might choose this method, because it will offer you a certain amount of extra control over your formatting, particularly if you have used a lot of pictures. The .mobi file structure, which is the native format for Kindle Readers (thought NOT Kindle iOS or Android apps) is a derivative of HTML.

A couple of very significant upgrades have been introduced in the last year, which make the HTML conversion process virtually irrelevant for most of us.

Firstly, the latest version of KDP's online conversion engine is dramatically better than it was, and is very capable of converting your Word, Open Office, or Pages (.doc or .docx) file without your help.

Secondly, there is little or no reason why you need to use the Downloadable Previewer any more, because the Online Previewer has also improved a lot.

If you're publishing fiction, without illustrations or any clever or special formatting requirements, the process is really simple. If you are publishing non-fiction, which may include illustrations, bullet points, numbered lists etc, you need to pay attention to the rules which Kindle imposes. These vary from version to version and the formatting procedure is constantly improving, so we will use the most updated version as of October 2014.

E-Book Publishing Software

There are various third-party e-book publishing software programs that you may be tempted to try, such as PubStar. In my experience, these generally over-complicate the process, and are completely unnecessary if you have access to a decent WP programme such as Microsoft Word, Apple Pages, or Open Office Writer, which is free. However you have created your manuscript, you should build a clean version of your whole book as .doc or .docx file using either Word, Pages, or Open Office Writer, and this is where we will do the bulk of the checking and editing.

Getting Your Manuscript Ready

The first thing you need to know is that any fancy formatting that you include in a WP document risks being lost in the conversion to Kindle format. If you choose to make a career as a Kindle author, you may want to study formatting in more detail, because there are elements of control which you can exercise (using HTML) which will enhance the way that your manuscript is displayed on various Kindles and third party device Apps. However, as we've said from the beginning, this book assumes you're a novice and that your objective is to get yourself published on Kindle quickly and cleanly.

In terms of time planning, you should allow a full day to go through this publishing process. You may complete it very quickly, especially if you're publishing a novel which doesn't have any formatting issues. However it's worth spending some time if you are publishing non-fiction, to get the best possible formatting before you publish. Apart from the various Kindle dedicated devices, there are also Kindle App's on Apple's IOS and Google's Android, and these behave slightly differently to the authentic Amazon machinery. Getting an optimum format from a single manuscript for all devices can be tricky, especially if your book is complex. Using common sense to iron out any major formatting variations is the best way forward.

Uploading to Kindle

Before you start the upload process, you should gather all your information together in one place. Once you start the process, you can break off at any time and return to it later. However, if you prepare well, you can complete all the steps in one short process.

This step-by-step process is intentionally simplified here, to give you a feel for what is going to happen when you do it for real. It should be read in conjunction with the next section, which goes into more detail about how to work with the KDP Previewer, once you have the process underway. Read them both, then come back and start the process from here.

The Dashboard

Open your KDP screen and log in to your account. Choose *Bookshelf* and click on *Add New Title*.

Book Name

The first thing you will be prompted to enter is your *Book Name*. This should be the Title and Subtitle you have decided for your book, in exactly the way you would like it displayed on your Sales Page.

Series Number

Next, is your book part of a *Series*? Probably not if this is your first book, so ignore it. If you write more books, you can change this easily in the future.

Edition Number

Ignore *Edition Number* at this stage.

Product Description

Next is *Description*. This is the only place where I usually break with convention. This is the 'Blurb', which is going to appear on your Sales Page, and it is extremely important. Writing your *Product Description* is covered in detail in the Marketing Section. When I publish a new Kindle book, I normally write a 'holding' description in this box during the first pass, and while I am waiting for the book to go live on Amazon, I go back and spend a few hours writing a really good Product Description, and then go in and upload it separately.

This is purely psychological, and for me it's about getting myself into a different 'Marketing Mindset', which I prefer to do once I have settled down from the intensive editing and formatting process. I like to download a real copy of my book onto my Kindle and iPad and read it just like a genuine customer before I feel able to really get to grips with the Product Description. Here we're talking about maybe one day's delay in having a finished Product Description up on Amazon, so it doesn't affect Sales.

For now, just write what comes into your head, check the spelling and grammar, and move on.

Contributors

Next comes *Book Contributors*. The simple rule is not to give any credit away. If you wrote the book, and nobody else made a serious contribution, don't add anything here. But if you promised to mention your Editor or your Illustrator, now is the time to add them. It won't appear on your cover or inside your book, but it will appear on your Sales Page.

There's an irritating trend of late, which is authors loading additional keywords in as Contributors in order to try to game the system. Whilst this may or may not have a minor effect on your search ranking (if it looks too good to be true, it usually is) but it looks tacky and unprofessional on your Sales Page, and could be off-putting for some potential buyers. Therefore you shouldn't do it.

Language and Publication Date

Set your *Language* (the default is English) and enter a *Publication Date*, as previously discussed. If you leave this blank, KDP will assign the publication date. You can add any date you like.

Rights

Section 2 asks you to confirm that you are the rights holder, so check the *This is Not a Public Domain Work* box.

Next Choose your *Categories*. You can specify two, and you should. When you click on *Add Categories* you'll be presented with a bewildering list of options. The best way to choose these initially is to look at your competitors and see which categories they are selling in. This is shown on each book's Sales Page in the data block just above the Reviews.

Many non-fiction buyers don't search in Categories, preferring the route-one method of entering their requirements into the Search box instead. But some do, and also your Ranking in your Category will be shown here, and that's a serious credibility factor when people come to choose a book to buy. It's not just kudos if you get to be in the top few of your category; it can really boost your Sales. But more importantly, it contributes to your Page Ranking, so if you get up towards the top in your category, and that category is close or identical to the major keyword that people are searching on, you'll be towards the top of the Search results.

If you get to be Number One in a particular category, you'll see a 'Bestseller Badge' displayed alongside your book, and this is a huge boost to your sales, so choose carefully. There's more about Categories in the Marketing Section, and you can come back and change this setting later. Unfortunately, Amazon's categories can be a bit of an enigma, and you'll need to keep a constant check on where your book is featured, because Amazon may sometimes re-categorise your book without any consultation. This can be frustrating, but you can exercise some control over it by remaining vigilant.

Choosing Amazon Categories

You should ideally complete this exercise as part of the Preparation phase before you get to the Publication process, however if you didn't, you can do it now in a different window on your PC.

Go to Amazon.com. Change the drop down on the search box to "Kindle Store" and click "Go" without typing anything in the search box. Next, look in the navigation column on the left and click on your Category to open it and double-click down to your chosen Sub-Category and click on it. The results that will fill the page will be the Best Sellers and the newest books in your Sub-Category. Look at your ten best-selling competitors. Open up their Sales Pages and scroll down to *Look for Similar Items by Category*. Make a list of all your competitors' Category paths, for example:

Kindle Store > Kindle eBooks > Nonfiction > Self-Help > Motivational

and *Kindle Store > Kindle eBooks > Nonfiction > Self-Help > Personal Transformation*

Choose the two that are used the most by your top competitors.

If the last term in a Category path is included in the Category menu of your Dashboard, choose it (the main Category may be different from the one in the Amazon store navigation Category path). Amazon is full of idiosyncrasies in Categories. This is because there are standards in the book industry, but Amazon ignores them wherever it can.

If your favourite competitors' Sub-Categories are not visible in the Category menu of your Dashboard, leave one of your two Category slots blank when you publish, and then use *Contact Us* at the bottom of your screen, and request Amazon to put your book into the appropriate Sub-Category and Main Category.

To calculate the approximate value of a Sub-Category, look at its Best Seller. If it has a Best Seller Rank lower than 25,000 (10,000 in UK), that Sub-Category is probably not very profitable. Conversely, if you are more interested in getting a Best-Seller badge quickly, placing your book in a category like this will certainly make it easier to get to the top of the pile. You can always switch categories later, once you have that badge (and a screen-shot to prove it).

Enter Your Keywords

Next, you can enter up to seven keywords. We covered keywords in an earlier section. Keywords are another very important element in your Marketing process, so pay attention to this and make them count. These keywords are considered as part of your book's *metadata* (the bunch of tags and details that are used by various search and ranking functions) and you will rank *somewhere* in every search that is made on these words.

Upload your Cover

Next you will upload your book cover file. This should have been saved as a JPG file earlier, and it's best if you stick to KDP's recommended size, which is 1560 x 2500 pixels. If you upload a file that does not meet these parameters, KDP will either reject it, or worse still will re-scale it to fit their dimensions, which can look dreadful.

Digital Rights Management

As mentioned elsewhere, I'm not convinced that DRM has any significant effect for low-volume books. If you enable DRM, it should help to ensure that your book is protected against pirates who might steal it and make it available for sale or distribution on non-Amazon sites. There are a million reasons why this is a bad thing, so if you care about it, don't give them the opportunity.

Personally, I leave it unchecked unless an author I am working with specifically requests it.

Upload your Manuscript

Next, you will upload your book file by Browsing and selecting the final file name. You can upload your original .doc or .docx manuscript document and KDP will reformat it accordingly. Alternately you can upload an HTML file, which is really only useful if you have included some advanced HTML formatting. These options are explored in the next section.

Shortly afterwards you will see the KDP system performing the Conversion and it should return a Green Tick to tell you that the conversion has been successful. It will also spell check your manuscript and tell you if it finds errors. If there are mistakes you will be given the opportunity to inspect the file, and you'll need to make corrections.

The Online Kindle Previewer

Now you can view your book in the Online Previewer, which you should do. This version allows you to see all the different Kindle devices as well as the Apple iPhone and iPad, which is really useful. Go through each device and look at as many pages as you can find time for. If you see any serious formatting issues at this stage, you'll need to fix them in your original manuscript, and repeat the upload process with a new version of your file. Once you are satisfied, click back to your Book Information in the top right corner. There's a complete and detailed explanation about this part of the process, again in the next section.

At this stage, you also have an option to *Download HTML*, which will return to you a converted version of your manuscript. If you are interested in using HTML, you might want to download this so you can use it in the future. Of course you can go back into the dashboard and get a copy any time you like.

Save and Continue

You now have a choice of *Save as a Draft*, which allows you to move onto the next stage without committing the information, or *Save and Continue* which will upload all the information you entered to Amazon and start the formatting and approval process ready to construct your book's Sales Page. If you select *Save as Draft* you can come back shortly and change things if you wish, but you cannot proceed to the next stage until you click on *Save and Continue*.

Territories and Publishing Rights

The Second Page starts with Section 8 where you select your publishing *Territories*. Unless you have a specific reason not to do so, choose *Worldwide Rights*, which will ensure that your book goes up on all Amazon websites. Alternately you can choose from (currently) 245 territories. If you do this, your book may be visible to some people who are unable to buy it.

Royalties and Pricing

Section 9 is about *Royalties and Pricing*. This is discussed in greater details elsewhere, but here are the key considerations;

First you will see a new feature, called *KDP Pricing Support*. You can go explore this if you have a few minutes to spare, and you'll see what Amazon 'recommends' you set your prices to. I recommend you ignore this. At first glance, it appears to be a very helpful function, however I am suspicious for two reasons;

Firstly, the system doesn't take into account the size and quality of your book but appears to search only on other books in your category. So in this sense, it's hard to see how the comparison can be truly equal.

Secondly, the system doesn't appear to differentiate between self-published and independent authors versus the big publishing houses. Of course JK Rowling can get $10 a book, but you cannot (you can try, but it won't work). For these reasons, I recommend you ignore this tool.

So, having dismissed it, you can now plunge in and start setting your own prices.

If you want to promote at 99c/77p, which is always a good place to start if you want to persuade lots of your friends and relations to download your book, you will need to select the 35% royalty option. You can come back any time and change it, but the minimum price that Amazon will allow for the 70% royalty option is $2.99.

If (for some unknown reason) you want to price your book above $9.99, you will also have to choose 35%. I don't think this is important to you. Above $9.99 you won't sell many books unless you are promising miracles or revealing the location of buried loot!

Next you can enter your pricing and see how it will affect your Royalty. Even if you select the 70% option, some of your sales will default to 35% on Amazon.com if they are outside the main Amazon territories. This is a minor consideration for most books. For amazon.com (the first box) choose the USD price that you like. I recommend $2.99 as a starting price if you are not using 99c as a promo.

If you want, you can leave the other territories checked and Amazon will calculate your non-U.S. price accordingly. For most territories this is probably not very important if you're writing in English. However, the UK market is substantial, and likes £1.99, £2.99 etc. In the UK and European territories, Amazon adds 3% Value Added Tax (VAT) to the price you specify, so if you want your book to be on sale at £1.99 or £2.99 (or more) you'll need to divide by 1.03 and round down to the next penny in order to account for this VAT imposition.

My preference is to manually set my prices for the US, UK, and the four European markets, but let Amazon set the other territory prices automatically, based on the USD price.

Kindle Matchbook

Section 9 is about *Kindle Matchbook*, which allows people who already bought your print book to obtain the e-book edition at a discount. The lower limit for your Paperback price to enrol your book in Matchbook is $5.99, in which case you can select $0.99 as the Matchbook price, and you will receive the 70% royalty rate on any sales made this way. Here's a stat: out of the last 10,000 books I sold on Amazon only two opted in to Matchbook, so you can probably ignore it at this stage.

Kindle Book Lending

Section 10 is to enable *Kindle Book Lending,* which allows Kindle owners to lend the book to their friends or family. For this to work, your book needs to be enrolled in KDP Select, which is covered in detail in the Marketing section. For now, this is inconsequential, so enable it (just in case it makes Amazon like you better).

Save and Publish

That's it. All you need to do now is tick the disclaimer box below to confirm you agree the Terms and Conditions. If you still have items to complete in this screen or the previous one, you can select *Save as Draft* then go and finish what you need. If you are ready to go, click *Save and Publish*.

Now go and have a drink. You'll receive an e-mail from Amazon once your book is live on the site.

The Kindle Online Previewer – Your Best Friend

Here is a more detailed explanation of how to use the Previewer during the upload process, to check and correct any formatting issues that you spot. I make no apology for any repetition; this is the single most important part of ensuring that your book is of the necessary quality to impress and attract buyers. As mentioned elsewhere, the majority of self-published books on Kindle don't do this well. So it's a chance to differentiate *your* book from the pack.

As I mentioned, in the last year I have gradually abandoned the downloadable previewer because the online version is good enough. Once I've entered the title information and the metadata as a new project, I like to start the process by taking my manuscript exactly as-is and uploading it to the KDP dashboard. Once you have done this, KDP will perform a conversion, which takes just a couple of minutes, and then you can Preview Your Book in Section 7 of the first page of the dashboard.

Don't be afraid to play around in the KDP dashboard. It's non-volatile, so nothing you do is going to 'go public' until you tick the final *publish* button at the end of the process. You cannot break anything!

The Kindle Previewer will open your book, and you will be presented with an 'emulator' screen, usually set for a Kindle Fire HD. You can scroll through your pages and see how it will look on that particular device. If you have any formatting in your original manuscript, such as headings, numbers, bullet points etc., these will normally carry quite well into the emulator for display on the Kindle Fire, however you may notice some anomalies with headings. We will correct these shortly.

Scroll all the way through to become familiar with how your manuscript looks. You may also notice that any diagrams have reduced in size, and again we'll correct this shortly. When you've scrolled all the way through, slide back to the first page and we will have a look at how your manuscript will display on different devices.

Previewing on Different Devices

Kindle Devices

At the top of the window, click on the *Devices* tab and then on *Kindle E-Ink*. The Kindle E-Ink devices (standard Kindle readers) are the most prolific Kindle devices on the market, but not everyone has the most up-to-date version. However in my experience the Kindle E-Ink makes easy meat of reformatting even a badly formatted manuscript. Using the Previewer you can see how your book will look on a standard Kindle screen. The default font display is Size 3, and if you click on the **Aa** button at the top of the screen you can adjust the font size just as you would if you were reading on a Kindle. Once again scroll through the manuscript and notice what looks good and what doesn't look so good.

Previewing for IOS (Apple Devices)

The final family of devices that you can preview is IOS, for viewing on Apple iPhones, iPods, and iPads. In older versions of the Online Previewer, you were unable to view these devices on screen, but that has now changed. You simply select the device, and then scroll through exactly as before.

Should you wish to load your manuscript onto an iPad, for editing or reviewing purposes, this can be done using the downloadable previewer, which can convert your manuscript to .azk format, which you then "side-load" onto your own IOS device for viewing.

Bear in mind that the iPad massively outsells virtually every other tablet device, including Kindle, and that it's widely used as an e-book reader. So if you want to be 100% certain that your formatting is suitable for reading on an iPad (iPhones are less widely used for reading) you might want to preview your book on a real Apple device. If you own one, that's great. If not, try to find someone who can help you with this.

The process for viewing on Apple devices is quite simple, but it requires several steps.

- First, you'll need to use your WP's *save as* function to create an HTML file of your manuscript.

- In the Kindle Downloadable Previewer, and select *open book* and select the HTML file you just saved.

- The Previewer will take a few moments to convert your file to.mobi for Kindle. Once this is done, open up the Previewer and you will see a Kindle Fire screen with your your book in it, almost identically to the online previewer.

- Click on the *Devices* tab and select *Kindle for IOS*.

- A dialogue box will appear telling you that the Previewer is converting to an **.azk** file format, and after a few seconds it will confirm that it has completed the task.

- If you now use your Windows Explorer or Apple Finder and go to the folder where you stored your original manuscript and your HTML file (the one that the Kindle Previewer has been using so far) you should find a new folder called *Converted-(name of your file).htn*. If you open this up you will find a couple of files in there, and the one you're interested in is the .azk file.

- Now you need to get this file into the Kindle app on your iPad or iPhone. To do this you will need to sync your Apple device with your computer using iTunes. You may be set up to do this by wire or wirelessly. For simplicity we'll assume that you're using a wired sync.

- When your Apple device is connected to your PC (or Mac), iTunes should open. If it doesn't, you should open it manually. Once iTunes recognises your device you will see it appear in the left-hand column, and if you click on it you will be able to see the status of your device in the main window. If it starts to sync, just ignore it: it doesn't matter.

- Click on the *Apps* tab at the top and when the window opens, scroll right down the screen until you can see *File Sharing*, which lists the apps on your device that can transfer documents between your iPad and the computer. Click on the Kindle App, assuming you have it on your iPad. If not you can to download it free from the App Store before you start this process

- The recommended method now is to shrink the iTunes window so that you have it open alongside the File Explorer window which shows the location of your .azk file. Drag the .azk file into the iTunes Kindle documents window and it will appear there. Hit the *Apply* button at the bottom of the screen and then the *Sync* button.

- On the iPad, open the Kindle app and look in the Library and you should see an icon for the file you have just transferred. If you touch it, your book should open on the iPad, and you can now scroll through it in the same way that you did using the Kindle Previewer on your computer.

Doing it this way is a little time consuming, so only do it if you really feel the need. The advantage (when you're editing) is that you are now able to read your book exactly as it should appear once it's published for real, and you have all the Kindle App functions, such as highlighting and notation, which can be really useful for your final proofing.

You can probably see that the formatting on the iPad screen is different to that which you previously saw on the Kindle Previewer screens. Don't be disheartened by what appears to be a lot of complexity in this process. In a moment we're going to go into your original manuscript and take care of the various standard formatting items which will ensure that you optimise the book for display on each of these devices.

Now that you are familiar with the Kindle Previewer and how to preview on IOS, you can repeat this process as often as necessary through the formatting procedure. It's all about creating a balance to ensure that readers on different devices get a good experience. Your readers will make allowances for the odd line or two out of place, but if your manuscript is a mess they will punish you in the Reviews, which is not what you want. So it really is worth spending some time on this, and by trial and error getting where you want to go.

But, to repeat, these days the Online Previewer is very good for all devices, and unless your book is complex you should not need to get involved with the Downloadable Previewer.

Managing Preview Files

Once you have been through this process the first time, I recommend that you delete the .azk files and their containing folder because you won't be needing them again. You're going to create new ones each time you run the test. As a general recommendation you should constantly delete files that you are only using for temporary purposes, so that you don't get confused

Fixing Formatting Glitches

Whether you're using Microsoft Word, Pages, or Open Office Writer for your editing, the formatting rules are the same. The menus might be in slightly different places, but are virtually identical in their execution across these WP platforms.

I recommend that you have the Previewer open in one window, and your WP manuscript open in another window alongside it. That way you can fix issues from the Previewer as you go through.

So, let's open up the manuscript and start fixing it.

- First remove all blank lines that serve no purpose.

- You should be using Page Breaks to ensure that each new Chapter starts on a new page, but you can get rid of any other Section Breaks which serve no purpose. If you particularly want Sections to start on a new page, just use the *Insert Page Break* tool.

- If you are using bullet point lists, try to avoid using indents as well. Make sure your bullet points are against your left margin, and the same goes for numbered lists. As you have seen, some Kindle devices will use indents wherever they see a line return, and this can make a mess of numbered lists and bullets. Without some in-depth HTML knowledge, you cannot eliminate this formatting on the devices that insist on it. The simplest way to alleviate the problem is never to use indents and bullets together.

- Try not to use centering. I know, I know, it looks nice for a Chapter Header but it will often look messy in the final product. If you use 'Title' headings for your front-page title, most Kindle devices will automatically centre it anyway.

- When formatting for Kindle, you don't need to worry about line breaks, widows and orphans, or keeping paragraphs together. Each Kindle device formats a different size page, and you just need text that flows without any intervention. Let the machinery do the work.

- If you're using tables, you can now construct these using your WP embedded table function. In older Kindle versions of software, it was necessary to use an embedded JPEG or GIF of the table, but the Kindle formatting software now recognises tables from WP programs, which is a much neater and tidier way to work. Just beware, because the Kindle Fire or iPad may sometimes not handle tables as you would like them. If you hit problems with this, convert your tables to graphics (pictures), which will be explained in more detail shortly.

- If you are working from an existing manuscript which may have been previously formatted for some other device, perhaps as a free e-book, or even as a CreateSpace manuscript, it may be easier for you to start by removing all the formatting and then working your way through and reintroducing headers etc. To remove all formatting in a document, use *Ctrl+Space+n* and this will remove everything, apart from carriage returns. You can view the remaining carriage return format by turning on *Show* or *Hide Formatting*, which is usually found in the *Paragraph* section of your WP toolbar.

Using Headings

Your word processing program offers you the facility to use different levels of *Headings*. You will see that if you highlight a line of text and click on a type of Heading, which is in the toolbar in Microsoft Word, the appearance of the text will change, and in some cases also change colour. Don't worry about the colour when you are preparing a Kindle manuscript, because everything will appear in black and white on monochrome Kindle devices, though it may pick up the blue colour on a colour screen device. If you explore the *Headings* options you will see that there are lots of different ones. For the purpose of preparing our Kindle manuscript we will restrict ourselves to using *Headings One, Two, Three, and Four*.

These different styles are part of the Cascading Stylesheets (CSS) functionality in HTML. This may not mean much to you, and you don't need to know about it: suffice to say that these designated headings are recognised in HTML, and as a consequence are recognised by the Kindle encoding process so that they will display properly when your manuscript moves onto the electronic reader screen. They also have another important purpose, which is to enable you to automatically create a Table of Contents, which in the Kindle environment allows readers to click through to particular headings.

For these reasons, you should definitely use Headings when preparing your manuscript. I recommend you use the *Title Header* only for the book title on the first page. Chapter headers can use *Heading 1*, major sections use *Heading 2* and so on.

When you come to create your Table of Contents, which is one of the final things to do before uploading the manuscript, you are able to select what depth of Heading you show in your Table. You can choose only to show (for example) the chapter names, or you can go as deep as every single sub-section in your manuscript. You should remember that a longer Table of Contents will take up valuable space in the *Look Inside* portion of your book.

Graphics and Pictures

At one end of the scale, a typical novel won't have any pictures or graphics, which makes the whole formatting task relatively quick and simple. At the other end, you may be publishing something like a Children's book, or a Comic Book, which are almost completely based on pictures and graphics. In either of these cases, KDP has a custom solution for you, in the form of its special *Content Creator* software. You can find out all about these great tools here:

https://kdp.amazon.com/help?topicId=A3IWA2TQYMZ5J6&ref_=kdp_BS_tool

However, if you are going to include pictures, graphics, or tables in a 'standard' Kindle book, there are some traps for young players.

Because the various Kindle devices and Apps have minor variations in the way they handle code, in particular how they position and display graphics, without some in-depth knowledge of HTML it can be tricky to get a consistent look and feel across all devices. Here are just a few of the things that can trip you up;

o   You cannot wrap text around a picture and expect it to display the same on all devices. Therefore you should always set pictures to *wrap in line with text.*

o   GIF is the ideal format for a Kindle picture, because it is the smallest file size format and won't impact as much on the Delivery Charge that Amazon levies on larger e-book files. If you are only using a few monochrome images, you will be fine with JPG's, which is the Kindle default when converting your pictures in the KDP engine.

o   No matter how you set up your .doc or .docx manuscript, Kindle will not accept centered images on all devices. On some screens it will shrink your image and left-align it. On others it will be bigger, and potentially force unnatural section breaks and page breaks on the adjacent text.

o   If you need to center an image which is smaller than the entire page width (for example a graphical Chapter header), use your graphics program to place the image centrally in a white or transparent rectangle (called 'padding'), then save the combined image as a GIF, at least 300DPI and at least 8" wide. This will ensure that when Kindle downsizes it to fit the various screens, it is still large enough to extend across the width of the page.

o   If your image is intended to be a full-page picture, make sure you insert a page break both before and after it in your manuscript, so that it won't cause any stupid line breaks when it's displayed on a screen which is longer (e.g. Kindle Fire) versus squarer (e.g. iPad).

o When you test your manuscript in the Kindle Previewer, if you are suffering inconsistent sizes for your images, here's a fix that works, although it's not the most elegant way to do it. I recommend this is the last thing you do once you have completed all the other formatting for your text and headers, and tested the upload at least once:

o Recreate your graphics as GIF's or JPG's, at least 300DPI, and at least 10" wide. Then save a copy of your manuscript in *A3 landscape format*. Ignore the page breaks, which will look crazy. Insert your images where you need them to be, as large as possible (the full width of the page is OK), then save as a new file and upload to KDP. This should now ensure that your images display full screen-width on all devices because Kindle will shrink them only as far as it needs in order to fit them on the screen. Remember, the actual page size you work on has no relevance to KDP; it simply sees the items on the page (text, graphics) and the paragraph and page breaks.

o If you are struggling with Tables, convert them to JPG's and handle them the same way. The quickest and simplest way to do this is to magnify your Manuscript page as large as possible on your screen, then take a partial screen shot, which will save your table as a JPG.

o On a Mac, this is done by holding CMD-Shift-4, then moving the cross hairs to encapsulate your table and letting go the keys. Your image will be stored on your clipboard, or alternately in Dropbox (another good reason to have it) from where you can rename it, download it, and insert it into you manuscript.

- On a PC, I recommend you download and install *Jing*, which does the same job but has its own dialog box to name and store your images.

- Never drag and drop, or copy/paste images. Always use *Insert Picture* or *Insert Photo from File*. I won't bore you with the reasons, but it won't work unless you do it this way.

Graphics on Kindle is a huge subject, but every version of the KDP conversion engine improves it a little. The key is to test first, then use the above methods if you aren't seeing what you want.

For the full story on how to work with images, pictures, and graphics in KDP, there's a great Kindle book by Aaron Shepard called *"Pictures on Kindle"* which does exactly what it says on the cover, and costs less than a Starbuck's Latte.

Review Your Progress

You've now been through your manuscript and fixed the headings, removed all the blank lines and inserted your indents or bullet points if you are going to use them. You're getting close to a final manuscript, so save it again as a new file. Upload to the KDP dashboard once more and open up *Preview My Book*. Choose the *Kindle Paperwhite* option.

Open up your Word Processing window with your manuscript in it, alongside the Kindle Previewer, then work your way page-by-page through your Kindle book and make any corrections or adaptations dynamically to your master Manuscript. You will notice that, if you removed all the formatting from the original manuscript, the Kindle device (in the Previewer) has taken care of right margin justification.

You can now see if you have any problems with bullet point lists, and you can take the appropriate action. Single lines of bulleted lists work fine, but if the text in a particular bullet point extends over more than one line, this may be where you will encounter formatting problems. Without HTML knowledge there's no simple way around this, so you need to use your common sense to decide whether the bullet points are really important, versus whether you think your reader will be able to live with the minor indiscretions in your formatting.

Make sure that you don't have any surplus blank lines. Make sure that tables are formatted correctly, which they should be. Make sure that you are happy with your headings and that you have used the right levels.

By the way, it doesn't matter what the page size is in your WP program whilst you are preparing a Kindle manuscript, Kindle will ignore it.

Front Matter

Front Matter is the generic term given to everything at the beginning of the book which is not part of the manuscript itself, for example: Title Page, Frontispiece Illustrations, Copyright Pages, Dedications, and so on. You can put pretty much anything you want in the Front Matter, but as has been mentioned before there are some considerations when publishing on KDP:

Look Inside

The First 10% of your book will be viewable in the *Look Inside* facility on the Amazon sales page. It's hard to over-emphasise the importance of this as a marketing tool, and therefore you should keep your Front-Matter to the absolute minimum necessary. It's quite understandable that having slaved for years over your manuscript, you may feel the need to have an outpouring of gratitude and explanation in the Front Matter of your book. Please take a step back and think about this carefully. If your main objective in self-publishing is to create a legacy, then go right ahead and throw in the kitchen sink! Conversely, if your objective is to sell books, *less is more.*

Front Matter Page Numbering

Conventional publishing advice is that Front Matter, i.e. everything which precedes the actual story or manuscript part of your book, should have different page numbering to the rest. You do not need to worry about this when you are publishing with Kindle, because the Kindle conversion system will take care of everything.

If you do nothing at all, Kindle will assume that Page 1 is the first page *after* your Table of Contents. So if you want your Kindle customer (after they have bought your book) to start at a particular place, bear this in mind when you choose the location for your Table of Contents. There are ways to *force* the book to start in a different place, but this requires you to mess around with HTML. If you are keen to learn about this, download a little book called *"From Word to Kindle"*, again by Aaron Shepard, which explains everything.

When designing your Front Matter, you do not need to re-invent the wheel. Grab a few books off your own bookshelf and see how they treat this stuff.

ISBN's in E-Books

If you are only planning on publishing your e-book on Kindle, there is no requirement for an ISBN number. Furthermore, you should definitely *not* include the ISBN number of your CreateSpace or other hard-copybook in your

Kindle e-book. Firstly, it serves no purpose, and secondly, this is actually against the conventions (and Amazon's rules). If you really want an ISBN for your e-book, you will need to obtain one from your national ISBN licensing agency. Frankly, unless you're going outside Amazon to expanded distribution, you needn't bother. Amazon will allocate an ASIN (the e-book equivalent of an ISBN), and you don't need to include this in your manuscript.

Copyright

In the old days, you had to include an elaborate passage of text regarding copyright. This is no longer the case since the USA changed their rules. All you need to include as a bare minimum is the following example: © the copyright symbol, and make sure that you use the correct one, which you can enter from the "insert symbol" command on your WP program if it does not automatically recognise the bracketed (c). This is a legal requirement should you ever find yourself in any kind of litigation over your copyright. Following the symbol, you should place the year, e.g. 2013, and then your name. Like this: © *2013 Rick Smith*

If you look at a conventional book, you will find lots of material about reservation of rights, assertion of rights as the author, and ordering and trademark information. You will also find details of the publisher's address and various catalogue numbers, which are there to enable bookshops and distributors to order and control stocks of publication. You do not necessarily need any of this in your book.

Here (once again) is the sample copyright paragraph you can use if you want something a little more elaborate.

"© 2013, [your name]. Except as provided by the Copyright Act [date, etc.] no part of this publication may be reproduced, stored in a retrieval system or transmitted in

any form or by any means without the prior written permission of the publisher."

Edition Numbers and Publication Dates

You may wish to place an edition number and other information about first-publication dates and so on. This is entirely up to you, and in my experience it has no bearing on the sales numbers of your book.

You can find comprehensive list of Front Matter parameters, and lots of other useful information about design, at www.thebookdesigner.com. I am not affiliated to this site.

Contact the Author

If you are publishing non-fiction, you may want to include some contact details in the front-matter. If you have a website or a Facebook page you should mention these. Personally, I include an e-mail address to enable readers to contact me with any comments or suggestions they may have for my non-fiction books. Although this may sound like a bit of a privacy risk to some people, my logic is that if I give the reader an opportunity to address me directly with any critique they have, it may offset their urge to write a negative review on Amazon. Conversely, if I received an e-mail saying how much people enjoyed the book (and this does indeed happen), then I have established a direct connection with a happy reader and I can direct them towards the review facility on Amazon. It makes more sense to keep communication private, especially if there is a risk that it may affect sales.

It also helps if you are building an e-mail list, which I heartily recommend and which will be covered in the Marketing Section.

Your Preface

When publishing non-fiction, the Preface is a critical part of your book, particularly because of the Amazon *Look Inside* facility. The purpose of your Preface is to give people a summary of what they are going to find inside the book, but also to excite them and stimulate them by picking out key reasons why they should buy it and read it. Potential readers and customers respond very well if they feel that you understand them, their issues, their challenges, their questions and so on. When writing your Preface you need to try to get inside the mind of your reader and think about why it is that they are looking for a book on the subject.

Successful non-fiction e-book writers tend to have a system, and you can model this for yourself. The elements of a successful preface are as follows:

Title your preface with a powerful statement. You might use terms like *"Secret Weapons"*, *"Inside Information"* or similar statements which give the potential buyer a reason to read on, because they think they will discover something that has value.

Next, a paragraph or two which creates empathy with the potential reader. You might describe why your book is different to others on the subject, and how you understand the situation that your reader finds himself in and the questions for which they are seeking answers. Also in this section, unless you are writing an expansive biography (*About the Author*) you may want to write a short passage or paragraph which establishes your credibility as an expert on the subject matter. Use phrases like *"based on discussions I have had"*, *"in my experience"*, and make sure that you are promising the reader something which they will clearly understand, and which will help them.

Next, you might include a bulleted list of the key points and discoveries that they will make if they read your book. I suggest you keep this list down to a minimum of five or six items, using words like *"how to" "discover" "learn"*, and keep each statement to a limit of one line, or two at the most.

Next, you may decide to include another bulleted list describing some of the reasons why people have failed in the past and the mistakes that they typically make in this subject.

Finally you close off the Preface with a reinforcing statement about how reading your book is going to provide them the answer is that they need and improve their life.

Write and rewrite the Preface, and spend time in getting it absolutely right. It's an extraordinarily important part of your book and your marketing strategy going forwards. By the way, it's completely unnecessary for a work of fiction.

If your non-fiction book is more along the lines of a history or biography, your Preface would then be more in the form of an introduction to the subject material, and your bulleted list may be a summary of the key events. One tactic you can use is to frame your list as questions in the first person, in other words try to emulate the kinds of questions that the reader is asking themselves whilst they search for a book on the subject: *"How do I?"* and so on.

How to Use This Book

The next important ingredient if you are writing non-fiction information books is the "How to Use This Book" section. This is a summary of the key actions that you want your reader to take whilst reading your book. You may tell them that they need to read it in Chapter Order, or that they can jump about and pick out the subjects that are interesting for them. You may describe the process that they're going to undertake, and explain to them how easy and simple it's going to be.

You might also describe why your approach to the subject is new or different from the way it's been done in the past. Finally you might choose to include a description of any additional resources that you're providing, and repeat the access information for your Facebook page or website. Personally I always sign off at the end of the How to Use This Book Section with my name, date, and my location. I feel that this helps me to create a stronger bond with the reader, and personalises the reading experience for them.

Then ensure that you leave a blank page, on which you may just include the simple title of your book half-way down, before you start the first chapter.

Back-Matter

Grab a couple more books off your bookshelf, and go directly to the back. What you're most likely to find there is promotional material for the author's other publications, and there's no reason why you cannot do this too. Whereas when you publish a hardcopy book by CreateSpace, you may be trying to keep the number of pages to a minimum in order to keep the price low, when you publish your Kindle book it's almost irrelevant if you add a few more pages at the end. But it's a great opportunity for you to further solidify the relationship with your reader, and hopefully sell some more books.

Promoting your Other Books

If your reader has enjoyed your book, they will probably come off the final chapter in a bit of an anti-climax. If it's a novel they may have become quite involved with the characters, and even if you've killed off everybody there's a short period of time where they will suck up anything else that you have written. So if you have another novel, you should definitely be promoting it on the very next page to the end of your story.

If you have a cover design for your other book, place a JPEG on the first blank page. I often use a black-and-white picture here, even if my cover is in colour. The trade-off is that I have a smaller file for which Amazon charges me less to download, but I know it will display perfectly on a monochrome Kindle device. The downside is that it will display in monochrome on a colour screen, but I figure that's a minimal issue, especially for the kind of simple covers used on non-fiction books.

If your follow-up book is another novel, you need to write some powerful Blurb, which would probably be the same as you will use on your Amazon Sales Page. In 200 words or less you need to wrap the potential reader into your next story. You can include a link to the Amazon sales page where they can buy the book, assuming that you already have it published. Please note that due to the ongoing rivalry between Amazon and Apple, links to Amazon may not work on an Apple device. The best way round this is to link them to a simple page on your website which then gives them another button to click through to your Amazon Sales Page. Alternately you can use a *link-shortening* service to create a custom link, using tiny.cc or bit.ly, which also gives you the opportunity to track any click-through traffic. There's more on this in the Marketing Section.

This is a prime opportunity to sell your next book to the same reader, and if they can get it just by clicking on a link, you will definitely make additional sales. Don't worry if your book is not yet ready: include the words "coming soon from".

You don't have too many options here, but at least you will let your reader know that you have other books in the pipeline. As and when you have them published, you can always go back and upload a new version of your Kindle manuscript with the links inside.

In my young adult fiction series (by Joey K) I have links to at least two more books in every one, and by tracking my clicks through tiny.cc, I can tell you that over 50% of my series sales appear to be as a direct result of this feature. If you really want to understand this in detail, I recommend *'Write, Publish, Repeat'* by Sean Platt and Johnny B. Truant.

For non-fiction books, the story is more or less the same, however it may be appropriate for you to include a sample chapter from another of your books (you're not limited to only one).

Inserting Links to Your Other Books

You can insert a shortened link directly to the Amazon sales page by doing this, either in your manuscript (bearing in mind the Apple restrictions) or on your Website:

- Go to www.Amazon.com, or your local Amazon site if you're not in the USA and you would prefer to direct your buyers to your local markets. You can put in both links if you want.

- Perform a search for your book and then open up its dedicated Sales Page. Make sure you are looking at the Kindle version, because that is the one you're trying to sell via the link.

- On the right-hand side of the page you will see *Share* and the various icons for Mail, Facebook, Twitter, and Pinterest. Click on the *Share* button.

- A box will open. Look for the **Link** and you will see a shortened web URL which is unique to your Sales Page. Highlight the URL and copy it. Paste the link into your manuscript.

- In your manuscript, highlight the pasted link, right click and choose *Hyperlink* from the menu. A dialogue box will open. There are two important fields here: at the bottom is the *Address* which is the link you have just pasted. At the top, there is the *Text to Display* panel which offers you the opportunity to rename the link with a "display name". It should currently be showing the same link address as the bottom box. I recommend you replace this with words such as *"Buy it Now on Kindle"*.

- Click OK and you will now see your new wording in hyperlink format within your manuscript. Just bear in mind that the re-named link won't be any use in a printed copy of your book; for CreateSpace you should leave the original link without re-naming it.

- This is just one example of how you can insert and rename links in a Kindle book. You can use this method to insert links to just about anything and anywhere throughout your book. Amazon provides you with this link-shortening facility, which makes things really simple.

Table of Contents

I usually leave inserting the final Table of Contents until the very end. If you're using Word, this is an automated process, but nevertheless if you're continuing to make changes to your manuscript after you have completed the Table of Contents, it can sometimes foul things up. When you create a Table of Contents for a print book, it automatically inserts page numbers based on the pagination, because this is what interests the reader when they get hold of your physical book. For a Kindle book, it's different. The Table of Contents simply creates a set of links which enable the reader to jump directly to specific places in your book. You need to deselect Show Page Numbers when you set up your *Table of Contents*.

I will remind you that the first 10% of your book is going to be visible in the *Look Inside* feature on your Amazon Sales Page. Therefore you don't want to take up too much space with the Table of Contents. From a marketing perspective, the Table of Contents is useful to give people an idea of what's going on in the book, and here you need to balance the need for elegance and efficiency against functionality, if you think that your book is of the type where the reader will need quick access to a deep level, i.e. sub-sections and below. My recommendation is (as always) *less is more*.

With Table of Contents, we're talking only about non-fiction books. There is no practical purpose to inserting a Table of Contents in a novel. You will sometimes open up *Look Inside* for a novel, and find a ToC which just says *Chapter 1, Chapter 2,* etc. I found one recently which had over a hundred chapters. What were they thinking?

Where to Place It

Different writers and publishers insert their Table of Contents in different places in the Front Matter of the book. My personal preference is to put it after the Preface and other Front Matter, so that it is the last thing before Chapter One. However, if you have an Introduction or a Preface written by someone from outside, you may prefer to insert the Table of Contents before that.

We talked earlier about the Kindle's automatic start point, which is usually your Table of Contents. Personally, I assume that the reader has seen my *Preface* and *How to Use This Book* blurb when they opened *Look Inside,* so it's not really important for them to read it again once they download the book onto their Kindle device. Kindle users know that they can easily slide back to the very beginning if they need to.

Inserting the Table of Contents is really simple on a PC, but less so on a Mac.

If you are using Word on a Mac, the process is a little bit 'manual', and rather than waste a lot of bandwidth here, I recommend you look at this video on YouTube, which explains exactly how to do it.

http://www.youtube.com/watch?v=8WvmVZkGlow

If you are using Word on a PC, the process is completely automated, as follows:

Place your cursor where you would like it to be inserted, in this example just before the Chapter Header for Chapter One, and from the *References* menu at the top of your screen, click on *Table of Contents* to review your options. From the drop-down list click on *Insert Table of Contents,* which will open a new dialogue box giving you a number of options.

Firstly deselect the *Show Page Numbers* tick box because this is irrelevant in your e-book. Next go down to the *Show Levels* selection box and choose the depth of heading that you want to include in your Table of Contents. You will see from the panel on the upper right side that this Table of Contents feature recognises the Headings that you have selected in your WP program.

If you have stuck to our protocol and used *Heading One* for your chapters, you can make sure that only the *Heading One* links will show in your Table of Contents by selecting number 1 in the *Show Levels* dialogue box. If you increase this number you will see that you show more sub-levels of heading. When you're happy, click on *OK*.

You will now see a Table of Contents magically appear. Don't be concerned if there are items that you do not need, for example things you have inserted in your Back Matter. Just highlight them and delete them.

If you find when you insert your Table Of Contents that you're unhappy about some inconsistencies in the book, go down the correct them and then come back to your Table of Contents, right click anywhere on it, and select *Update Field* and your changes will be reflected in the Table. Sorry, this won't work Word for Mac, so you'll need to be fastidious about getting your Headings right, before you make your Table of Contents.

Manuscript Preparation Summary

Don't expect to hit gold first time or even second time. It may take you several tries to get to a result that you're happy with, but it's worth the effort. When it comes to getting reviews and increasing your readership, little things make a difference. You just don't quite know what those little things will be until your book hits the market!

Now, you've created your manuscript, you've taking care of your Front Matter and your Back-Matter, it's time to give your WP document what is hopefully your final check before you shoot for an up-loadable file for publication.

Once you have it, save it as another new version, and upload to KDP as before.

Test Again in Kindle Previewer

As before, open up Kindle Previewer in one window and open up your WP file alongside it so you can make changes whilst you review. Remember, the methods described in this book are intended for people who have no HTML skills, so you are looking for optimum results using only the Kindle Previewer and your WP program. If you have HTML skills, you have the ability to exercise a great deal more control over the appearance of your manuscript. There are books available that can give you this insight, and there is also a lot of information on the KDP Community and the Forum site under *Kindle Publishing Guidelines.*

I have published dozens of books on Kindle without any HTML knowledge whatsoever, and I have never received one single adverse comment about my formatting in the Reviews.

You can check and test your manuscript as often as you like until you're happy that you have an optimum file ready for upload.

Now you can carry on and set your rights and pricing, as described in the previous section.

9 – Building Brilliant Amazon Sales Pages

You'll remember that we entered a 'holding' description in the Product Description section during the upload process. Now it's time to go back and get stuck into this vital task for real.

Introduction

Each book sold on Amazon, whether an e-book, paperback, or other format, has an individual Sales Page, a single web page on each Amazon site. This is the store-front for your book. Once someone arrives at your book's Sales Page, you have 'qualified' them as a potential buyer. On the Sales Page, they should find everything they need to make a decision to buy or reject your offer.

Once you upload your book (hopefully both formats, CreateSpace and Kindle) you will need to set up your Sales Page(s) for maximum effect. On your Sales Page there are four main elements, each of which needs to be tuned up to absolute perfection in order to achieve the highest possible hit-rate. These are:

1. Your *Product Description* (the first thing they'll see and read).

2. Your *Reviews*

3. Your *Author Central* information (or a shorter *About the Author* paragraph)

4. The *Look Inside* feature, which is accessed by clicking on your Book Cover.

Product Description

The first and most controllable element of this is your *Product Description*, which you were prompted to enter when you went through the final process of preparing your upload on the CreateSpace and/or Kindle websites. As we said at that time, if you have simply typed in some 'holding' information, you can now get to work on reworking your Product Description, ready to upload to your Sales Page via the 'Bookshelf' function in KDP.

Think Like Your Customer

To understand the importance your Product Description (sometimes referred to as 'Blurb') you need think like your potential customer. If they have reached the point of reading your Product Description, it means they have done their initial search and chosen your book, based on its title and cover, and clicked through take a closer look.

This is gold dust for an Amazon author. Once a potential buyer gets to your Sales Page, they have probably made a decision to *buy* a book, and yours is a serious contender for their hard earned cash. Now your job is to convert them and make them hit the *"Buy Now With One Click"* button, so the deal is sealed.

So long as your Reviews are in decent shape, your Book Description carries enormous weight. For fiction and non-fiction writers alike, it is the most important and best opportunity you have to sell your book's content and messages, so you must pay close attention to it.

Check Your Competitors

Before you set about writing your Product Description, it's always a good idea to take a look at your competitors, and see how they've handled it. When you look at other Sales Pages, you'll notice two distinctly different types of layout for the Book Description.

Advanced Formatting

Some Product Descriptions will contain advanced formatting, such as orange coloured headers, italics, bullet-lists and bold type. If done properly, these formatting additions can be very appealing, and will often help boost your conversion rate, because readers naturally associate such sophistication with big publishers, which adds untold credibility. Text formatting can also be used to draw the eye to important statements in your Product Description.

The bad news is that the only way to achieve this kind of formatting is to insert HTML code inside the text when you are managing your book's information during the upload or revision process. I said at the beginning of this book that you would not need HTML in order to publish great books on Amazon, however if you want to format your Book Description in this way, it's unavoidable. The good news is that there are plenty of people who can do this for you at very low cost, for example on fiverr.com. Alternately you can do it yourself if you're careful, even if you have no HTML knowledge at all. In October 2013, Amazon made some changes to the HTML tags they will support, so if you get it done externally, you should ensure that your contractor is up with the latest play.

The best news is that there is a fantastic software tool called *Better Book Tools* (www.betterbooktools.com) which costs $47 for the complete suite. This programme converts your

Product Description text into Amazon-approved HTML without you needing any HTML knowledge whatsoever. The software also includes some excellent supplementary tools for keyword search and comparison, but for the HTML conversion alone I recommend you check it out. I am not affiliated to this company.

However, not all the big books use these methods, as you will see if you take a look at J K Rowling's "The Casual Vacancy", which has a Book Description which is done exactly as you will do yours if you just type (or preferably prepare offline then copy/paste) into the Kindle upload screen.

How Long Should Your Description Be?

Your Book Description can be up to 4000 characters. Some gurus advise you to use it all, and some say keep it short, especially for fiction writers. I've often been tempted with my 'How-To' books to try just posting "It Does What It Says On The Tin" when I'm worn out after a long writing session, but so far I've resisted the urge to experiment quite so drastically.

Realistically, you need to use just as much as is necessary to close the sale. If your Kindle price is low (say 99c - $2.99), the potential customer is in an 'impulse purchase' frame of mind, and will click through to buy your book once they have crossed the threshold of being convinced that it's worth the tiny financial risk. Conversely, if your price is high (say $4.99 and upwards), they may take more convincing, so the longer you can keep your potential reader engaged, the deeper you will immerse them in your book's 'culture' and the more likely they are to buy it. The exception to this is if you manage to turn them off with ridiculous claims, or bad grammar, which is a cardinal sin in your Book Description. If you have any suspicions about your own competence, you should ask for help and get someone you trust to check your Product Description before you upload it. Bad blurb will send your buyers scurrying away, and there are lots of temptations scattered around your Sales Page for them to click through to something else.

Shortly we'll talk about Author Central, which is useful once you have more than a couple of books live on Amazon. One of the facilities which Author Central promotes is the ability to control all your Product Descriptions from a central point. Avoid it like the plague, because once you start to use this facility you will find it becomes restrictive and inconvenient, for reasons we will explore later. Stick to uploading a Product Description for each book independently.

What to Write

There are some general points you should employ for both Fiction and Non-Fiction Book Descriptions.

Think Like a Publisher

Write your book description as if you are a copywriter who has been hired to do the job. You've read the book (goodness knows you've certainly done that) so you should understand everything about it, but you also need to step outside the process for a moment and describe the book as if you're trying to sell it to somebody. It's all too easy to be so immersed in your own work that you lose your objectivity. You must write your Product Description in the third person, and you must tell the reader only what they need to know in order to convert the sale.

Stay Away From Detail

Your job is to intrigue and entice the reader, not to give them a short-course in what you have written. It's invaluable to see what your competitors are doing. As a short cut, I don't think there's anything wrong with copy/pasting the Product Description from a book you admire into your WP, and then changing each sentence one at a time so that the underlying structure and flow are maintained, but the plot, content and characters are yours.

Grab Your Buyer

Grab your buyer at the start and always leave them wanting more. The first and last lines of your Product Description are the most valuable, and you should spend the most time on these. I'm sure, especially if you've written a thriller, you've been through this process for the first sentence of your book, so get into that mindset again and write a devastating opening line.

Close the Deal

Always end your Product Description with a *call to action*. In every kind of selling situation, potential buyers need to be told to *do something* or they will often carry on browsing somewhere else. This is called *decision support* and you shouldn't omit it. There's more about this at the end of this section.

Fiction Descriptions 101

I'm not much of a fiction writer (well not yet anyway, I have to pay the bills first) so I've gone out to the wider world to see what the experts advise is the best way to approach fiction blurb. Here's my interpretation of what I learned;

Set the Scene Powerfully: "When Rick Smith sat down to write once more on that fateful Monday Morning, little did he know the maelstrom of chaos that was about to unfold in the days ahead..."

Briefly Introduce your Key Antagonists, Scale, and Environment: "Ten thousand miles away in the Australian Outback, evil forces were preparing to unleash events of catastrophic dimensions that would change Smith's world forever..."

Link It All Together: "Unwittingly catapulted onto an explosive trajectory that would see his very soul pulled apart, as he struggled to contain a terrifying sequence of events that threatened to destroy not only him, but the entire New Malden Book Club..."

And Summarise: "How would it all end, or could it really end at all?"

Did you see what I did there? OK, that might not be the best fiction blurb ever written, but I'm sure you get the drift, and if you look at a few more Book Descriptions in your specific genre, you should find it much easier to come up with a good one of your own!

Non-Fiction Descriptions 101

Writing a non-fiction Product Description is completely different. Here you are trying to convince your reader that they'll be making the best possible decision by buying your book, in order to answer the questions or solve the problems that brought them to Amazon in the first place. You need to get inside the mind of your customer, and ask yourself the same question.

Here's a break-down of the Product Description structure I've used for my book "Master Self-Hypnosis in a Weekend" which is in a highly competitive sector and is sitting high up on the first page in Amazon:

Why My Book Is Better Than the Others (the Passive/Aggressive Approach): "Hundreds of books have been published about Self-Hypnosis, so what makes this one special? Well, maybe you're trying Self-Hypnosis for the first time, or maybe you've tried before and failed. Whatever the case, you're looking for *results*, otherwise you'll probably waste a lot of time, and come away disappointed and disillusioned. You need a System."

Clarity of Explanation and Implied Guarantee of Results: "In 'How to Master Self-Hypnosis in a Weekend' professional hypnotist Rick Smith demonstrates a step-by-step system which anyone can use to succeed."

What's In the Package?: "Everything you need, included freely downloadable script recordings, is provided. Using this book, you will quickly master the key Self-Hypnosis techniques that enable you to drop easily and quickly into a comfortable trance anywhere, anytime."

How You Will Benefit: "You'll also learn how to use your new Self-Hypnosis skills for relaxation and recreation, how to use Self-Hypnosis to control stress and to centre yourself professionally, how to attack bad habits, such as smoking, drinking, over-eating, in fact anything that you feel the need to change, and how to empower yourself for motivation, focus and commitment."

The Short-Cuts That Will Save You Time/Money/Frustration: "You'll also discover how to avoid the common mistakes that other people make: they don't practice often enough, so they fail to master the key techniques; they don't get the 'set-up' right, so they become distracted; they cling on to their inhibitions, so they never release their restrictive self-control; and they try to analyse too much, rather than allowing nature do its best work."

How It Will Be For You Once You Have Read It: "If you follow these step-by-step instructions you will quickly learn everything you need to know in order to master the simple skills of Self-Hypnosis. With regular use, you will acquire a powerful secret weapon that will serve you in almost any aspect of your life. And the more you do it, the better you will become."

Sign Off: "It's easy, it's quick, and it's really fun to do! "

You can use bullet-point or numbered lists for some of your factual statements, but you'll need to use the simple HTML tricks to get them to display well. You should also add a Call to Action such as *"Buy it Now"*, or *"Click on 'Look Inside' to Find Out More"*

You'll also notice a liberal sprinkling of Keywords throughout this Product Description. On no account be tempted to write a long list of keywords and put it at the bottom of your Product Description. This is such an obvious attempt to game the system that I am convinced the Amazon 'crawler' that indexes your book will ignore it. And it looks (once again) tacky and unprofessional.

Let It Cook

I'm so arrogant and confident that I reckon I'm the best grammaticist I know, so it's rare for me to show anyone my Book Description before I upload it. However I always let it cook, at least overnight, then come back and polish it a couple of times before I'm ready to commit. I've also been known to change it half-a-dozen times in the first few days of publication, because just like your book, you never really get the true flavour for your own creations until you read them in the real context and environment. Don't let this scare you: it's important that you don't let details like your Product Description slow you down from publishing. The beauty of Amazon's platforms is that you can easily go back in and change anything you like, at any time, and within a few hours all trace of your previous follies is gone forever, apart from the copy stored on GCHQ or the NSA's spy servers!

If you are inexperienced as a writer or communicator, it's a great idea to give it to someone else to read. The simple questions you're asking are: *"Do You Get It?"* and *"Would You Buy It?"* Make them read it in front of you, and only once or twice, because that's the way that your potential customers will read it, and they won't dig in to discover deep meanings. You only get one shot with an Amazon customer, so you'd better make it count.

Although it sounds obvious, just run it through your spelling and grammar checker before you post it on the site. You won't be the first person who unwittingly published an accidental howler, and it will definitely be spotted by the public at large.

Using Your Blurb on Your CreateSpace Back Cover

There's not much difference between the Product Description you write for your Amazon Sales Page and the kind of blurb your publisher would have written for the Back Cover of your book if you were publishing through conventional bookstore channels. They both do the same job, which is to give the reader a summary of your content and a good reason to commit to buy your book. So if you're building a three-part cover for your CreateSpace book, you can recycle your Product Description for that purpose, maybe adding an author mug-shot to spice it up a bit.

When someone clicks on '*Look Inside*' from your paperback Sales Page (which might otherwise be identical to your Kindle page, depending on how the customer arrived got there) it's worth knowing that the back cover of your paperback will sometimes appear in the viewing window as the last page of the *Look Inside* section. On some browsers, it's possible to 'spin' the cover shot in order to view the back cover. However, the resolution of the picture is so low that it's usually unreadable.

Author Central

Amazon provides an additional option called Author Central. This can be very useful for a number of reasons, but you need to understand its implications before you commit, because there are certain restrictions which cannot be easily changed later.

Author Central is a Dashboard which allows you to set up a Biography, including Pictures and Videos, all about you and your work. Author Central also co-ordinates all your Book Sales Pages in one place, and allows you to control your Product Descriptions from a central point. If a customer clicks on your Author Name on any of your Sales Pages, they will see your Author Central page and a list of all your books, which they can then access one at a time.

For a fiction writer, Author Central is an excellent way to lead readers from one book to the next. For non-fiction writers in a specific genre or niche, it can serve the same purpose. For non-fiction generalists like me, Author Central is less useful. If your various books are unrelated, you may derive little benefit from connecting them this way, and indeed you may confuse your customer.

If you browse through some Author Central Pages, you'll come across wide variations in quality. Many amateur writers seem to use the biography section to pour forth their passions and prejudices, perhaps not realising that their potential readers may be turned off by statements like *"I am first and foremost a Mom"* or *"I have been committed to Scientology since an early age"*. There's nothing wrong with holding views, but it can be unprofessional to put yourself out there in this way. You need to make your own decision on this, but it's hard to see how it will ubiquitously help your sales.

When it comes to Page Control, there are some time-saving features in Author Central, but it can also lead you into problems if Amazon changes the rules, which they do from time to time. Recent variations in HTML standards between Author Central, Createspace and KDP have caused many authors some serious headaches, and if you manage your Product Descriptions from Author Central, your allowable word-count will reduce from around 7-800 words to less than 500. This might not be important for you, but it's always a good idea to keep your options open. Even worse, once you commit to managing your Product Descriptions on your Sales Pages through Author Central, you cannot then revert back to managing them directly in KDP's dashboard.

You will find that Author Central also allows you to add additional copy blocks to each Sales Page, like *From the Author* and *From the Back Cover* which may entice you. Frankly, if you've concentrated on writing an effective Product Description, you could undo a lot of good work by indulging yourself in these 'opportunities'. If your customer can't make a decision to buy your book based on your Product Description and *Look Inside* offerings, I don't think that another few hundred words are going to make much difference, so I would avoid them.

It's doubtful that Author Central will serve much purpose until you have a few titles in play, so at this stage I recommend you simply make yourself aware of its existence, and ignore it until you are much further down the line.

"Look Inside"

The *Look Inside* feature has come up in several sections of this book, which underlines its critical importance. *Look Inside* is designed to replicate the experience of browsing in a bookshop. A bookshop customer would rarely buy a book only by its cover. They would flick through a few pages to get a flavour of the content, but more importantly the writing style. People will not buy books that are hard to read. Your central job as an author is to create content which flows easily for your reader. Difficult, over-fussy or verbose text is a big turn-off.

The *Look Inside* feature displays the first 10% of your book free. We talked in the Formatting section about how you shouldn't waste too much of this portion with unnecessary Front Matter, Dedications, and so on. There's a huge element of impulse purchasing in the commitment to buy. Amazon knows this better than anyone, which is why they introduced '*Buy Now With One Click*'. This button is repeated in the *Look Inside* pop-up which appears on screen, so it's a reasonable bet that if you can't get your *Look Inside* prospect to buy it from that screen, you'll have lost them to another title.

Don't worry if you didn't pay too much attention to the *Look Inside* section whilst you were finishing your original manuscript, because you can easily upgrade it any time, and upload a new version via KDP or CreateSpace.

To describe this first 10% as critical is not understating the fact. But even more so, the first few paragraphs are acutely important, because your style and readability will be judged within the first twenty or thirty seconds. For this reason I have made repeated recommendations that you stay away from anything self-indulgent. When a reader starts looking at your *Look Inside,* section they may be turned off by self-serving biographies or irrelevant contextual descriptions. Be Brutal.

I often read and review up to twenty books a week, as a part of my participation in author communities. Unfortunately, at least half of these books are badly written in some way or other, and poor grammar is the biggest turn-off. It takes no more than two paragraphs to form an opinion about a book, so even though you may think that the whole ten percent is important (which it is) the first page is pivotal to sealing the deal.

You will recall from an earlier section that I impressed on you the need to own a Kindle Reader or an iPad, so that you can read your own book just like a customer, and here it is really important. Once you have your book on your own screen (not your computer; that's too much like your manuscript) you must read and re-read your first few paragraphs, and be super-critical about the quality and conciseness of your writing. The question you should be asking yourself is *"Would I buy this book based on the first page?"*

Do whatever it takes to ensure this early text is world-class. That's not to say that the rest of the book can be sub-standard, but this little section matters most of all in the sales process, because if they don't go any further, or click on the *'Buy Now With One Click'* button, you've lost the sale.

Summary

That's it! If you've followed all the steps so far, you are now a Published Author. Congratulations!

That may well be enough to scratch your itch, but if you're interested in making some money from your book, you'll need to do at least a little bit of Marketing, which is covered in the next section.

SECTION 3 – MARKETING YOUR BOOK

Introduction

So, that's the easy part done. You've written your masterpiece, you've worked your way through the publishing process, and now it's time to set about promoting and selling copies. This is where many novice self-publishers struggle, because they think that Marketing is a dark art.

It's unlikely that your book is going to sell itself, so you need to be pro-active about promotion. Luckily, Amazon puts you on a level playing field with the blockbuster best-sellers, so it's up to you to take advantage and exploit the opportunities that are in front of you.

10 – Powerful Marketing Mindset

If you're setting out to be a serious self-publisher, you'll probably have another book idea in the pipeline already. So the first thing you need to do is organize your time between marketing your existing book and writing the next one. Everyone has their favourite aspects. Some people love the creative process but can't get their heads around the things they must do to make a commercial success of their publishing. Some people just don't care very much; they've achieved their ambitions simply by finishing their book and seeing it out there in the public domain.

Perhaps you could look at it this way: once you have reached this stage of the process, you have finished your *product*. Unless your book is highly time-sensitive and requires constant updating, you have created a valuable asset which should now endure for years without any further effort. So, as far as this book is concerned, you're free to focus all your attention on promoting and selling, so that you actually make some money out of it!

Your Marketing Objectives

It's a good idea to set up some disciplines about how you will split your available time between your marketing efforts and writing the next book. There are two main ways you can grow your earnings with self-publishing:

- Selling more of the books you've written, and

- Writing and publishing more books.

The good news about writing is that once you've been through the creative and publishing processes, the next time will be quicker. You'll have fully understood the tasks you need to execute. Hopefully you'll have been down all the blind alleys, made all the basic errors, and learned the lessons. If you're a fiction writer, there's no real short-cut to writing the next novel, because nurturing and birthing a 100,000-word quality story is a major undertaking. However, if you're writing in the non-fiction genre, you'll have understood how to organize your workload by using the tools we explored in the earlier sections. These days, I find I can generate a new book in less than a month, even if it's an unfamiliar subject.

Get Started

My system is to take a week immediately following the publication of a new book, to throw myself into the marketing before I start the next one. The most important stage in marketing is to create some initial momentum and see a few copies going out of the door, then you can build up the intensity of your activities, and eventually they'll become semi-automated and take on a life of their own. The key to Amazon is to get yourself up the Search Rankings, so that your cover appears on the first screen when people search for your subject or keywords. Once you have things rolling you can split your time between marketing and writing. Have no doubt; the time you spend on promotion and marketing will earn you more money in the long run. But that doesn't mean you can ignore your new project.

If you're writing full-time, you may find that a simple splitting of your days, for example Marketing in the Morning and Writing in the Afternoon, works best for you. If you find yourself to be more practical in the mornings, this is definitely worth considering. When I was in business management I made it a rule never to make commercial decisions in the afternoon, because my sugar levels changed through the day and I always found more practical logical focus in the mornings, whereas my creativity would unleash itself after lunch.

If you're fitting your new writing business (and it is a business) around your day-job, then you may find that you can write well in the early mornings, before real-life takes over. But whatever you do, you must not neglect your marketing, and it doesn't have to be onerous.

The profits you pocket will be the difference between the gross royalties you receive from Amazon and the money you invest in promotion. So, unless you've actually written a blockbuster first time out, you'll need to be circumspect about your marketing budget.

Ordering Your Own Book

We talked about the different ways you can get hold of your book once you've published it. Because you've used CreateSpace, you need to lay your hands on a few paperback copies straight away. Here's what you should use them for:

Family and Friends

You need to give a copy to anyone that you consider assisted you whilst you were writing it. Of course that includes people who may have given you practical or technical assistance; they will expect a free copy as soon as it's published, and it's much more effective and memorable to give them a real signed copy than simply have them download it for their Kindle device. The more copies you can put into peoples' homes and offices, where they might show it or lend it to someone else, the more you're going to sell by natural word of mouth and networking.

But don't get carried away; if you start handing out books willy-nilly you'll soon run out of cash! You need to toughen up and get into the mindset of a professional author. People will understand that you're in business to make money from your books. I carry a few copies whenever I go out to a professional gathering or club meeting, and if people ask me for a copy, I sell it to them for less than the cover price but more than my cost, so at worst I break even. I'm able to obtain my normal books in bulk from CreateSpace for about £3.50, shipped to me in the UK, so I sell them for £5, which is pocket-money for most people, but I make a big song and dance about personally writing a nice message in the front and signing it.

Believe it or not, friends and acquaintances often buy more than one. People always attach significantly more value to something they bought than something they were given, and some people take pride in saying to their friends that they know the author, so don't be afraid to ask for at least enough money to cover your costs. If you live in North America, the pounds will convert to dollars, because you'll save so much on shipping costs. So you'll be buying your books for about $3.50 and you can easily sell them for $5, especially if the Amazon sales price is around $7.95.

Review Copies

We'll talk about how to seek out reviews in the press and media later, but you'll need a few copies for Reviewers, which you will have to give away. Even though professional reviewers will always prefer to obtain your book on their Kindle (they have to read a lot of books), which is easy to arrange by 'Gifting' through Amazon, you can kick-start someone's interest in your book and create a sense of obligation by presenting them with a pristine paper copy at the beginning. It's definitely worth a trip to Staples to pick up a pack of No.1 Jiffy Bags for sending your books out!

Raffles and Prizes

If you belong to any organisation that has social or fundraising events, you should always put at least one of your books "Signed by the Author" into the Raffle prize pool. People will read your book if they choose it from a prize table, and they may even lend it to someone else to read if it's not their cup-of-tea.

There are lots of other reasons for you to ensure you always have at least a few of your books handy. Never miss an opportunity to place a real book in the hands of someone who might read and recommend it to their friends. This is the art of Networking, and it's really cheap marketing.

The worst thing you can do is order a large quantity of your paperbacks at the beginning. Buy only as many as you need, according to the plan you make for the above categories. The main reason for this is that you may update your content or your cover in the near future, and you don't want to be stuck with a huge box of outdated editions in the trunk of your car (where most of these boxes end up).

Go Carefully

If I have a title which I'm unsure about, or perhaps something which is in a really tight niche, I don't bother ordering direct from CreateSpace, but rather I buy them in blocks of five from my local Amazon website. You need to work out the economics of this, depending on how you've priced your book for sale. Remember, you will earn royalties on these sales, so the actual price you pay in the end may not be too much more than the Author Copy price, plus you'll get them in a day rather than having to wait, which is a major advantage if you're based in Europe. For some strange reason, even after your book is available Print-On-Demand in the UK, Author Copies are still shipped from the USA, and this adds anything up to a month and a couple of dollars to each copy.

Plus there's an added advantage of buying your own books through Amazon, which is that the Sales show up in your Amazon Rankings, which is important to help you gain some initial sales momentum. Of course you can buy as many as you want in paperback, and they'll all contribute to your ranking, whereas you can only ever own one Kindle copy, and deleting and re-purchasing is a dubious practice. I look on the incremental margin that I pay for buying them this way as a legitimate marketing investment, and of course you can charge the whole cost of the books against your tax bill, assuming you're self-employed. And regarding tax, here's some important information you need to know if you're a non-US author:

US Tax Treatment of Royalties

You may never discover this information unless someone tells you or you read about it on the KDP forums. All Royalty income from your books is declared to the Internal Revenue Service (IRS) in the USA. Amazon's arrangement with the IRS is that they must deduct US withholding tax at 30% from all overseas payments to authors, unless you have personally made an arrangement to be exempted, and confirmed that you will declare your royalty income to your home tax authority.

The W-8BEN Form for Tax Exemption

Until mid-2013 (and this may still be the case for some nationalities) this involved downloading form W8BEN from the IRS website, completing it accurately, then submitting it back to Amazon for them to process on behalf of the IRS. The process is now taken care of electronically on the Accounts section of the KDP website, and you should see a pop-up box when you first set up your Kindle Authors Account. Don't ignore this, because they will keep 30% of your royalty income, and you will have an enormous job ahead to get it back from the IRS. The critical piece of information that you need to obtain is an Employee Identification Number, which is issued by the IRS on application, because without this they will not process your application and confirm your withholding tax exemption. Let me be clear: you need an *EIN*, not a *TIN*, which causes a lot of confusion.

Obtaining your Employee Identification Number (EIN)

You obtain your EIN by telephoning the IRS in the USA on +1-267-941 1099. An operator will handle it for you over the telephone and issue your number there and then. They'll tell you it takes a few weeks when you first speak to them, but if you clearly state that you are an Amazon author, and answer all their questions satisfactorily, they will give it to you over the phone. Be prepared: the usual on-hold time to get through the system is an hour or more, so it's advisable to use Skype or it will end up costing you a fortune for your call. You must call during US working hours (East Coast) and anecdotally it seems to be quicker if you call in the afternoon. Don't be put off by the official nature of the operator. If you've ever been to America, and dealt with TSA or Homeland Security at an American airport, you'll know that the US government apparently trains out all traces of humour in its civil servants. The downside is that they won't appreciate any jokes or comments you make whilst you are on the call (typically British behavior), but the upside is that they are ruthlessly efficient and if you follow the process, and answer the questions correctly, you will always get exactly what you need. Remember, they are real people doing a job. Treat them with respect and you'll get the result you want.

Once you complete the formalities with Amazon, you'll receive an acknowledgement by e-mail that your case has been completed and your exemption granted, and this will ripple across both your KDP and CreateSpace accounts. By the way, on this subject and any other issues you may have with Amazon in Seattle, their Customer Services staff is extremely helpful and friendly whenever you contact them by e-mail.

Promotions &
8299 & 99¢
for XMAS → January

11 - Pricing for Profit

Pricing Kindle E-Books

If you've just spent months (or even years) writing your masterpiece, it may be tempting to try to translate your efforts into *your* perceived value for the finished book. It's an easy trap to fall into, especially if you're viewing this exercise as your life's work! But beware: there are lots of really great books out there that never do any business for their authors because they're priced too high.

The simplest objective when self-publishing any kind of book is to move volume. Let's really simplify the equation. If you had a notional target to make a thousand dollars from a book (it doesn't matter over what period of time for the sake of this exercise) it's far better to sell a thousand books and make a dollar on each one than it is to sell a hundred and make ten dollars on each one. You have created your product so there's no incremental cost, no matter how many copies you sell, and it makes sense to try to grow your fan base rapidly by 'stacking high and selling cheap'.

The massive market you (usually) want to address is the USA, so we'll talk in dollars for now. If you go onto Amazon.com and Search for the books in your category, you'll see a vast range of prices. If you refine your search to '*price, low to high,*' you'll see several 'bands' of pricing.

First you'll see the *Free* books. These are usually books that are enrolled in KDP Select, and are using their five-day free promotion 'allowance' to get exposure and generate reviews. We can ignore these titles for now, because we have no idea what their authors' plans are once they come off free promotion, and neither do we know at what price they were selling before their promotion began.

also possible that Amazon has dropped the price to zero, because it has *'price-matched'* that book against another Sales Channel (such as Smashwords). Amazon reserves this right through its agreement with you at the beginning, so be aware of it. Some authors use this as a deliberate tactic to get a book permanently listed for free on Amazon. Ignore this for now; you may want to use it later when you're more experienced and you have alternate strategies, but for now, stay away from alternate channels and stick to Amazon's price rules, if you want to earn money.

KDP Select and Free Books

Amazon operates a programme called 'KDP Select' which you are invited to join through your KDP dashboard when you are preparing your book for publication. The simple advice is this: KDP Select requires you to make your book exclusively available on Amazon for 90-day periods. There are other e-book distribution channels (Smashwords, iBooks, etc.) but they collectively do a fraction of Amazon's business and I have not yet found anyone who makes serious money through these channels, though Apple's iBooks is growing quickly. So I recommend you accept the exclusivity clause and Enrol your book in KDP Select right at the start. You'll gain several advantages;

Firstly, Kindle customers who subscribe to *Amazon Prime* will be able to borrow your books for free, and you'll get paid each time this happens.

Secondly, your book will be included in the recently-launched *Kindle Unlimited* program, which is covered in more detail shortly, and which is proving to be a serious volume factor for many categories, especially kids fiction.

Third, you'll be able to run five days of free promotion in every ninety-day period. All these opportunities are covered in more detail later in this section.

Fourth, if your book is in KDP Select, you will receive the 70% royalty rate across all Amazon's main markets, whereas if you aren't, some markets restrict you to 35%.

I also believe (anecdotally) that Amazon mildly favors authors who sign up for KDP Select. I have no solid evidence to prove this, and I'm sure that if it's true, Amazon is never going to admit it. However, amongst the hundreds of independent authors I am connected to, the ones who seem to have the most customer service issues, such as disappearing reviews, are not in KDP Select, but are distributing across other platforms too. I have all my books permanently enrolled in KDP Select, and I have never experienced any of these issues.

The Price Ladder

Next you'll probably see a lot of books priced at 99c (77p). There are a few different reasons to price a book this low. Firstly, it may be a very small book. Have a look at the data halfway down the Sales Page for a few of these and you may see that they are just thirty pages or less. Well done to these authors, who have understood the value of their short works, and priced them accordingly. Amazon gives a good clue here, with their 'Singles' category, which are usually Short Stories. Some people like these, especially if they are following a particular fiction writer who pumps out these short stories at a quick rate (some do this very successfully). If you have a short book like this, 99c should be your price point, at least at the beginning. Of course there are exceptions to every rule: if you have a ten page book called 'Alchemy - How to Turn Lead into Gold', then clearly the information you're selling is much more valuable, and even if it's only ten pages you can probably command a higher price. But until you write that book, stick to the rules.

99c is also a really good alternative to free promotion, because every sale is a sale, and even at 99c it will contribute equally to your position in the Amazon Sales Ranking, so if you are trying to get up onto the first search page in your category quickly, promoting at 99c is a good pitch. Just bear in mind that if you publish a short book, the *Look Inside* feature may cut off before the reader gets anywhere near the serious content, and this is a big turn-off.

So there's a good chance that a lot of those 99c titles are actually more valuable books that are recently launched or looking for a boost.

99c novels sell well in the holiday season, particularly in the female categories (RomComs, Mummy Porn, Period Drama etc.) because fans of those genres will often load up their Kindles with several cheaper titles before they head off to the beach or pool. 99c pricing alone is not going to make you successful without a great cover and some well-written blurb, but you'll see a lot of these types of books in that price bracket. You need to know that if you price at 99c, you can only select the Amazon 35% Royalty arrangement, so don't think that you're going to leave your pricing there unless you start to see some amazing volume (it has been known).

Next you'll see books priced between around $1.65 and $2.99, which is the beginning what we'll call the 'sweet spot' for e-books. $2.99 is a great price point, because you can select the 70% royalty deal, which will earn you over $2 for every copy sold. $2.99 is also an attractive price for buyers, because it sits in a category called *impulse disposable income*', that is to say that people don't think too hard about clicking 'buy' if they see something they like at that price. It's

216

less than a drink in a pub, or a decent App on iTunes. If you're targeting a middle-class audience, around $2.99 is the place to be. It's the lowest price you can select in order to qualify for 70%, and in my experience it's the point where the lines cross between royalty revenue and acceptable volume.

Next you will start to see books priced up to $3.99, which is the notional upper limit of pricing for an unknown author who has something of quality to offer. $3.99 is a great price point if you are in a relatively small niche without too much competition. I have trialled a couple of my niche titles by switching between $2.99 and $3.99 after I achieved Top-10 status in my category, and after an initial dip when I raised the price, there was no noticeable difference in volume. At $3.99 you'll be earning around $2.70 (once file-delivery charges are included), and once you start moving tens and twenties each week, you start to see that the numbers become interesting.

After $3.99 the sky is the limit. If you're seeing titles at $6-$8, immediately discount the known authors because they are being controlled by mainstream publishers, who will set the pricing according to what the market has shown them they can achieve. They may also be protecting paperback and hardback sales by narrowing the differential. The big publishers are reticent to upset the high street book retailers by cannibalising paper book sales with e-books, because they need the Barnes and Nobles and Waterstones of this world to stock and sell their long-tail titles, such as high-cost photographic books, hot Christmas biographies and so on. You're not in competition with these books.

You may see, especially if you are writing in the *Self-Help* or *How-To* non-fiction genres, relatively unknown competitive authors selling up around the $6 - $7 mark. When you see these books, take a look at their Rankings. If they are in the Top 20,000 Paid on Kindle, then you're looking at a force of nature; a book which is selling big volume at a high price. Of course we all want to be there, but you can bet that the author, if he or she is self-published, has done a lot more than just write and upload a manuscript. They may have done serious PR, such as TV, Radio and Press interviews, which will massively boost any book. They might have found their way into Book Club recommendation lists, or any one of dozens of other 'professional' promotional tactics. What's almost guaranteed is that they didn't just get there by luck. At the very least they have captured a set of keywords which are bringing them up in every search, possibly as a result of choosing that magic title, such as "How to Get All the Sex You Can Handle" or something equally stunning!

But generally, self-published books above $3.99 don't sell a lot of volume unless they're unique.

Launch Price Strategy

It's hard to use generalisations when there are so many different combinations of subject, title, author and audience, but I would recommend you set a pricing strategy for your Kindle Book as follows:

Start at 99c, and accept the 35% Royalty deal at the beginning. Your objectives are to:

- Sell some copies, so climb your category rankings

- Get some reviews (more about that later)

- Do some online promotions

- See some moving figures, for your own motivation

You might run at this price for between a fortnight and a month, depending on how active and intensive you intend to be on your marketing and promotions.

Move up to $2.99 once you gain some traction. By this time, you'll need at least seven or eight five-star reviews, and to have established your Amazon on-line presence by refining your Product Description, and perhaps upgrading your cover. See how this affects your sales volume. If you see a dip at first, don't be alarmed, especially if you're in non-fiction. You might have some hangover effect from people that browse regularly and put you in their Wish List, then see your price go up and walk away. But you'll probably see your sales pick up again after a couple of weeks, so you'll know you've got it right. Stay at $2.99 for at least two months, and establish your position on the first page of your category.

It's worth pointing out that there's not much linear effect on Amazon. When people come in on a particular day for a book, they don't log prices and check back to see if they're going up or down. Your potential customer is with you for a fleeting moment in time, and there are millions more customers coming onto the site every day, so don't be worried about experimenting with pricing. It's a fickle market, and you'll only gain or lose customers on that day, at that price. It won't affect or damage you for the long-term.

If you're happy with your income at $2.99 there's no compelling reason to change. Amazon attracts such a massive pool of buyers that you'll start to notice some consistency in your sales numbers. Tracking by week is dangerous unless you're doing big volumes, because there can be significant fluctuations caused by public holidays, weather, and all sorts of other things. But tracking by month should be steadier, especially if you're smart enough to factor in seasonality. Once your monthly numbers are stabilised, either flat or with an upward trajectory, you might want to trial higher pricing.

Price versus Volume

When you're tracking monthly, work out whether the combination of increased price and decreased volume is making you more or less money, because you could quite reasonably live with a 10% drop in sales if you ended up with a 25% bump in royalty income because of a modest price rise. Remember, on the 70% royalty deal you can add 15% to your royalty yield by going from $2.99 to $3.45.

I like the $3.99 price vicinity. In fact, my own testing shows that a slightly obscure figure such as $3.87 is marginally more successful. Modern consumers have instinctively learned to round-up to the next whole dollar, and $4 seems to be a cut-off point for most titles in most categories.

UK Author Pricing

Note to UK authors: If you set $2.99 as your US price, you may be dismayed to see that the Amazon.com sales page will show you a price of something like $3.48 when you look at your book. Don't be put off by this (many authors are, and end up compromising their price in order to adjust down for this anomaly). Amazon charges 3% Value Added Tax on all e-book sales in the EU, so when you look at Amazon.com from a European IP address, it will automatically add this VAT to the visible price. In some cases, it will add an even higher premium. Rest assured, American visitors to the site are seeing $2.99 and that is the price they will pay, because they don't have the same VAT arrangements.

For pricing your books on Amazon UK and the various Amazon European sites, if you want to hit the x.99 price point, you will need to calculate the input price using the formula: £x.99/1.03, then round down to the nearest penny or eurocent. You will then see your book appear on the Amazon Sales Page at the correct $x.99 price.

As far as UK and European Authors are concerned, my recommendation is that you just swap pounds for dollars and run with 0.99, 1.99, 2.99 and 3.99. UK authors have a huge advantage because the price point of £1.99 is within the 70% royalty category, and this can work quite well in the early stages.

Whatever you choose today, I recommend you only change your pricing at the beginning of a month. Unless you're doing big volume, your sales trends will be too small to measure over a shorter period.

Linking to Dollar Pricing

When you set up your pricing on your KDP dashboard, there's an option to let Amazon set the UK and International prices based on the US price. To save you working out currency exchange rates, this is a tempting option. However, even though it might make sense to you in markets like India and Mexico, where your sales are going to be minimal due to affordability and language, I recommend that you set your UK price independently of your US price. The UK is the second largest English speaking market, and if you are a British Author, you are probably going to make significant sales in that market because the competition is less. Many US authors don't even bother to list their books on Amazon.co.uk, so take advantage of this and operate tactically in the UK.

Apart from anything else, because the UK market is smaller, and because you live there and are likely to have more personal friends and acquaintances that you can use to help you get some early sales and reviews, you will probably climb the UK rankings faster, all other things being equal. So it makes sense to pay attention to your pricing in Britain.

Price Testing

Never forget; your objective is to sell more books. There's a lot to be said for testing different prices, but if you find a level at which you're achieving your objectives, don't mess with a winning formula. The time to start comparison testing is once you have multiple titles in play and you can afford to make the odd mistake or two without affecting the overall running of your business, if that's the way you're treating your writing. Generally speaking, volume trumps value, because the more people that buy and read your book, the more viral it will become, the higher you'll climb in the rankings, and the more reviews you'll get.

Testing High Prices

It can be very tempting to price your book high and 'see what happens'. If you're already at a high run-rate, you can try this for a week and you'll be able to see whether people value your book at its new price. You need to use some self-generated analytics to figure out if you're making more money, because you will definitely be selling fewer copies. And you need to keep on top of the monitoring and analysing, because your sample size may drop to the point where you start to lose Ranking. If you should inadvertently go into free-fall, you'll need to start the whole process over again to get back to the front page, which is always more valuable than temporary spikes in revenue.

Competitor Research

The method I use is to look for a couple of 'decent' books in my category, with a reasonable assumption that we are competing on at least one keyword, and who are promoting at 99c (or even free, if I can't find any paid promotions). Then I set up a little Excel table and log their price and ranking each day once they raise the price (which they will inevitably do).

Knowing what we know about the value of sales in overall Amazon Rankings, I'm looking to chart how quickly their Sales decline. For example, I'm currently tracking a book which competes with me on the keyword 'Self Hypnosis' and which I know was recently promoting at 99c. The author has subsequently raised his Kindle price to $9.95 (which is, in my opinion, much too high for the category, and also the quality of his book) but he has a lot of good reviews and his Sales Page is good.

The day after he ended his 99c promotion, his Ranking slumped from around 15,000 to around 60,000, and it has fluctuated +/- 15% for the last week, but with a marginal downward trend. I will plot his Ranking for another two or three weeks, and if it stays steady or decays slowly, as it is at the moment, then I can roughly calculate that his sales at this high price are earning him more royalties than if he was doing what I'm doing at $3.99, since I am in the top spot for that keyword and category.

Based on what I see, I might be motivated to try a month at something like $7.95. The essence of this test is to try to understand and leverage consumer behaviour, using someone else's risk to provide the justification. I've used this method before, and it's as solid as research gets, given that you don't have a lot to go on!

If you want to be truly scientific, you should be charting as many competitive books as you can find which meet the criteria. You have to search to find them, because many authors, and most publishers, don't operate this tactically.

Statistically speaking, you're monitoring the trends of cause-and-effect.

But beware: intensive tracking and data analysis can swallow up great chunks of your day, so try to keep it simple and concentrate on a subject for only as long as it takes to get a feel for what is happening.

Pricing for CreateSpace Paperbacks

Pricing your hard copies is an entirely different proposition. The royalty calculation is significantly different because there's a base-line production cost for your book, so the majority of the price is going to Amazon and CreateSpace. Although they're part of the same company, you need to understand that CreateSpace is merely a printer in this context. So they set a price to Amazon, and Amazon sets a price to you.

In the *Price Calculation* section of the CreateSpace Publishing Dashboard, you can play around endlessly with your pricing to see how your royalty is affected. The first advice is this: unless there's something specific about your book that lends itself to paperback more than e-book, your CreateSpace sales will usually be a minority of your overall volume, so although pricing correctly is important, the royalties are not going to make or break you. As we said at the beginning, you're publishing in paperback as a service to your readers and a part of your overall publishing strategy, although of course if you're successful overall, you could make a significant amount of money from both channels.

Taking into account your Kindle price (let's assume you've taken my advice and you're targeting $2.99 or £1.99 once your promotion is out of the way) I recommend that you launch your paperback at a price-point close to break-even at the beginning. There is an opposing school of thought which says that if you price your paperback high, people will see the relative prices on Amazon and think they are getting such a great deal on the e-book that they'll buy it more readily. I'm on the fence about this, and even if it's true I don't think it's amongst the top reasons why people will buy your book in either format.

Launch Price Strategy

The CreateSpace dashboard allows you to lower your price until it won't go down any further. At that point, CreateSpace are making their money, Amazon is OK with their cut, and you are getting nothing. But it's a good place to be for a promotional launch, especially if it comes in under $5 or £4, which is comparable to paperback prices in the High Street. If you're publishing fiction, especially pulp, you will massively reduce your sales potential in paperback if you rise above what people are used to paying for the known authors' works, so check out the prevailing pricing in your fiction genre, and try to match it if you can.

Pricing for Value

For non-fiction, you need to bear in mind the value you're offering, especially in terms of the number of pages. Kindle buyers might not mind too much if your $2.99 "How to Demolish a Greenhouse" is only thirty pages, but you can bet that a serious buyer will churn straight off your sales page if you try to charge them $6.95 for the equivalent paperback. Of course you can mitigate this by choosing a smaller Trim Size when you design your CreateSpace book, which will add pages, but in any case you can't really get away with much less than 100 pages in paperback, or the value chain simply breaks down.

Try to remember the motivation for doing the CreateSpace book in the first place, and perhaps forget about making

225

serious money. I publish all my books in ~~both formats,~~ and I sell more than 20% of my total volume in paperback. I have a pricing formula, which is to adjust my paperback pricing so that I earn not less than 75% of the equivalent royalty-per-book than I'm getting from Kindle sales. This sometimes pushes my paperback price up a little further than I would ideally like it to be, but if I reduce it to hit a paperback price point, the royalty drops down much quicker than the price because of the ratio between my cut and Amazon's, so even a modest price reduction would mean that I have to sell more books by a factor of ~~two or three~~ not to hurt my overall income.

Of course a lot depends on the type of book, and whether it has a greater appeal as a physical copy, in which case you can justifiably ask for a higher price. But for most of us, the CreateSpace publication is there for reasons other than being our main source of royalty income, so it's more about making it acceptable to the market than selling a shed-load of copies and making a ton of dough!

Whatever the case, I can tell you from experience that there's nothing quite so nice as the day you open your first Amazon delivery and hold your own book, printed on paper, for the very first time. And that has a value which cannot be measured in mere monetary terms!

12 – Powering Up Your Sales

Introduction

Let's reprise the steps you've taken so far, just to be sure you've covered all the bases before you press the Sales button.

Now that you've uploaded your book (I call it 'Giving Birth' and for a guy it's the nearest you'll ever come), and you've received the e-mail from Amazon telling you that it's available on the store, the first thing you need to do is to look at your Sales Page. You're allowed to take a couple of minutes to admire how clever you are, and to feel that little bubble of excitement in the pit of your stomach: You Are a Published Author.

Inspect your Sales Page

Next you should carefully inspect all the elements of your Sales Page to make sure they're the way you want them to be. How does your visual cover display? Can people clearly read the information on the front, well enough to understand what the book is about? Is everything in line? Are you happy with the colours?

Read your *Product Description*. Hopefully you checked it very carefully before you uploaded it, so there shouldn't be any grammar or spelling mistakes. However, is the layout satisfactory? Read it a couple of times to make sure that it makes sense, now that it's in the public environment. Remember, if you feel the need to change it you can easily do so, but each time you make changes from the Kindle or CreateSpace dashboards, you'll have to wait anything between four and twenty-four hours for these to flow through to your Sales Page. So if you're going to make changes, you should collect them all together and do them in one session rather than piecemeal.

If you've used HTML formatting, did it come out the way you wanted it to? It's not unusual to make an error or two with HTML, especially if you're inexperienced, and even a wrongly placed space can have a disruptive effect on the look and feel of your text.

You won't have any Reviews yet, so there's no point looking!

"Look Inside"

Are you happy with what appears on the first *Look Inside* page? Read your book, and try to put yourself in the mindset of a stranger seeing it for the first time. Does it deliver? Again, remember that if you find anything wrong you can go back and upload a new version of the manuscript, once you have made any changes. See how much of your book appears in the portion; you might be quite surprised. Unfortunately, without rewriting your book, there is very little you can do about this, so just remember the rule, which is that although your whole book should be *brilliant*, the first 10% should be *stunning*! If you're uncomfortable with the order of your Front-Matter, spend some time thinking about how you might want to rearrange things when you do your first revision.

If you've used Author Central, are you happy with the way your information is displayed? Remember you can change your Author Central information and it'll wash through to all the books you have for sale. This can be done independently of your book Sales Page.

Buy Your Book

The first thing you should do is to buy your own book and download it onto your Kindle or iPad. No matter how many times you read it in the Kindle Reviewer, you really need to read it as a customer. You'll be surprised at what a different perspective this gives you. The first time I published a book on Kindle, I totally hated it when I read it on my iPad. In fact, I posted three or four new versions of that manuscript within the first weekend, because it was only after I got myself into the mindset of a customer (and actually paid for the download) that I began to see some of the self-indulgent and spurious phrases I'd included in my writing. That was probably the biggest lesson I ever learned, and it has permanently changed the way I write ever since.

It's a strange phenomenon, but when you're immersed in creating the manuscript, you're very much in the first person: it's all about *you* and how you relate to your subject. With non-fiction, your customers don't give a rat's ass about you, provided they have the least the impression that you're credible in your subject. I discovered this when I read my book for the first time, and I had to go back in and seriously de-personalise an awful lot of text.

The fiction author may have an entirely different experience. I know fiction writers who become so immersed in their plot and characters that the first time they read their published story they just hate it. For an Author who's just written a novel, it's important to allow a few days to pass whilst everything cooks and the juices settle. Some people are shy about giving their story to their partner or a close friend as the first "beta-reader" so it may be a good idea to seek out friends of friends (controllable strangers) so that you can get an honest critique without any personal embarrassment. One lady I met who writes erotic fiction has never allowed her husband to read her books in case he asks her where she's getting her information!

Everyone's process is different, but it's likely that you'll want to go through these exercises over the first few days, before you start to invest any time or money in promotion. Once you've ironed out all the kinks (and remember nothing will ever be *perfect* for you as a writer) you can get started on generating some sales momentum.

Even if you've priced your book at 99c or 99p, it's highly unlikely that the public are going to beat a path to your door just because you've published on Amazon. There are exceptions, but they are very rare. If you should be fortunate enough to start registering sales in the first few days, I congratulate you. Seeing the numbers rise in your Amazon and CreateSpace dashboards is the best incentive I know to get on and write another book! If the numbers are serious, in the hundreds or thousands, I really think you should consider hiring me as your writing coach and paying me a percentage of your royalties!

For the vast majority of us, we'll have to do some work to get our sales started. There's no magic formula about how long it takes to get your book moving, but it's pretty clear that the harder you work the more successful you'll be, always assuming that your content justifies its position in its market niche.

Friends and Family

Obviously your first soft target is to sell as many copies and downloads as possible to your friends and family. They are the easiest to coerce, and unless you are a social hermit you should be able to drive 20 or 30 sales in the first week. This is important because if you're writing in a relatively uncompetitive niche, 30 sales in a week may be enough to get you up into the Top 10 ranking. You'll be surprised how effective this can be, especially if a few reviews flow in as well.

There's a point in the Amazon process, although nobody really knows where it is, when Amazon decides that your book is worth putting some of their effort into, and it starts to create some automatic momentum of its own. Remember, Amazon is not a charity. It's a business which wants to make a profit, and if it sniffs your product as a potentially profitable item, there are lots of small promotional channels which may start to impact positively on your sales.

One good example is the banner bar below your book description which shows *"Customers Who Bought This Item Also Bought"* and if your book is in a niche where customers regularly buy two or three books on the subject, you could start seeing your book down there quite early. Once you're there, you're reliant on other authors having failed to go through the fastidious steps that you have in order to make their Book Description and Sales Page effective; the first place people will go if they churn off a Book Description is to that list of similar books. This is another reason why cover design is important, because as you can see, those books are very small pictures indeed, and the ones that tend to get clicked will be the ones whose covers can be read in a thumbnail format.

Facebook

Once you've saturated all your real friends and family, the next best place to push out your message is on Facebook. On the general subject of Facebook, almost every Kindle guru you read will tell you that you should be working on creating yourself an "Author Platform" for your book or your writing business. Whilst there is nothing wrong with this, you'll find that Facebook, and social media in general, has a very low conversion rate when you start promoting your products. That's not to say that you shouldn't do it, but you definitely shouldn't waste an enormous amount of time on it. This is time that you can better employ promoting in different ways, or even writing your next book.

Set Up a Second Profile

If you have a personal Facebook profile, and like me you limit it only to people that you actually know, it may be worth considering creating a second Facebook identity. I have one called *Rick Smith Author* which exists solely to build a much larger base of Facebook Friends, many of which I have not and will never meet. There I make contact and build relationships with other writers who can help me with reviews and keyword bumps (more about that later), and people that I vaguely know but who I would not ordinarily have on my personal Facebook Friend list. I do not try to friend unsolicited strangers, but I rarely turn down a friend request if one comes in, unless it's from an obvious crazy!

I also use my Rick Smith Author profile to join writing groups on Facebook, where an enormous amount of collaborative assistance and support can be found. If you have enjoyed this book so far, and found it useful, please feel free to send me a friend request on Rick Smith Author' and as long as you have a picture on your profile which doesn't look too strange, I will be happy to accept you!

In order to set up a second Facebook profile, you'll need a different e-mail address from your original one.

Post Regularly

Once you have your alternate profile setup, you should post regularly with information about your books, and anything else that's vaguely related to your craft as a writer. Just accept that actually promoting your books through Facebook is probably not going to sell huge numbers, but at least you will be establishing yourself as a writer in peoples' consciousness.

Fan Pages

I also create a Facebook Fan Page for each of my books, and list these inside the book itself. I'm under no illusions that this will make me rich, but there are readers who want to establish a connection with you as an author, and it's a good place to post news about upcoming promotions and new books as you write them. Just bear in mind that if you post on a Fan Page you will only reach between 10% and 15% of the people who have clicked "Like". This is tactical on the part of Facebook, because they want you to buy advertising, which will reach 100% of your fan-base and also their Friends, if you spend enough money. Beware; you can burn a lot of cash very quickly for very little return if you try to market this way. However, I do advocate spending $50-$100 at the beginning to get a few hundred Likes on your first page, so that at least when you do send information out into the world, you have a reasonable assumption that it will hit a few people.

I have no way of measuring it, but I'm guessing that I will earn my $100 back over a few months, and at some point in the future I may need a receptacle to link back from another book or to another business venture. Investing in Facebook is a nice-to-have, not a must-have, so if you're writing on a tight budget, don't worry about it. There'll be plenty of time for that once the royalty cheques start appearing!

You'll read a lot from online gurus who advocate that anyone writing Kindle books (non-fiction of course) should be thinking about how to connect back to a website to sell more products to readers. This may be the case if you're in a specific sector, particularly the self-perpetuating environment of 'online information products', and there are a few people making a lot of money this way. However, with my diverse range of books I have not yet found a formula with which I am comfortable to try to extract more money from my readers. Who knows, you may have an idea, in which case I'm sure you'll go and buy some books on how to set up online information product websites, and of course you know you can embed links in a Kindle book to drive traffic that way.

You are an Author first and foremost. If you want to be an Online Entrepreneur, publishing books may be a good traffic generator for you, but you'll need to look elsewhere for instructions on how to do this well.

Generally speaking, your objective is to drive your book up the Amazon sales rankings so that you can get it onto the first page in any Search category, and then tactically raise and lower the prices until you find the point at which you earn the maximum money each month.

The Hustle

About Free Promotions

If you are enrolled in KDP Select, you are offered the opportunity to promote your book for free, for any five days in each 90 day enrolment period. Many first time authors use these promotion days, and if you infiltrate enough forums and free-book promotion sites, it's not unheard of to get several thousand downloads. But is there any value to this?

My view is that the effectiveness of free promotions is no longer of much interest to a serious author. Most people who download your book won't even bother to read it. A lot of them are just hoarders, the same people who have tens of thousands of free music tracks in iTunes and never listen to most of it. It's also unlikely that any of them will review your book, which used to be the other great use for free promos. Current thinking is that "99c is the new free". In the context of the Marketing 'Hustle' you can squeeze much more benefit from 99c promotion, whilst working a lot less hard, and probably covering your costs in the process.

For a new novelist, free promo is still a way to get your name and material out there, and if you have more than one book, getting your free title into the hands of prospective purchasers for your other titles is a valid tactic. But it's a shot-gun approach, and I seriously suggest that precision marketing (called *below the line* in commercial circles) is a better way to go. If you want to know more about free promotions, there's a massive amount of information on the Kindle Community forum.

The concept behind free promo's was that you could make it big, very quickly, and some people have, but most don't. If you're going to build profitable sales and a loyal following for your books, hustling is the most satisfying and profitable method, because you maintain your direct involvement. You need to convert your audience one book at a time. If you can make a hundred paid sales in your first or second month, which is not so difficult to achieve, you can expect a steady upward trajectory. In terms of your business, a hundred paid sales, even at 99c, is probably better than ten thousand free downloads in terms of run-on sales afterwards.

Hustling in the Author Community

The smart self-publishing authors are constantly working together as a group, partly to compete with the marketing muscle of the big publishers, but mainly because the best people to give you honest help and critique are people who are in the same position as you. There's camaraderie and solidarity to be found out there in the forums and groups, and you'll be made very welcome if you take out no more than you put in. Writing can be a lonely occupation, and having these collaborative relationships, even though they're only online, can be a great source of comfort and encouragement whilst you're trying to break into the business. You will also learn a lot because these authors are only too ready to pass on their experiences to newcomers. You will not be viewed as a competitor as long as you retain some humility in your dealings and don't start acting tough!

As I explain elsewhere, trying to market your books on Facebook is probably not going to work that well, but using Facebook (and LinkedIn for some people) to organically build a network of collaborators is a very worthwhile use of your time. And it's free!

It's important to stay within Amazon's Terms of Service (TOS) so you need to take some small precautions. The most important one is that if you provide your book for free to a specific reader, it cannot be in *exchange* for a review, and your reviewer is well advised to state that they received the book for free in any case.

As you'll have gathered, I'm not a big fan of free giveaways. Reducing your book to 99c (77p) is equally if not more effective, and although you'll move a lot less copies on your promotion, by attaching a value to your book you'll ensure that people take you more seriously as a writer and author. Also there's a much better chance that your customer will actually read your book. If they then review you, with no coercion, that is absolutely within the ToS.

A really great place to find other authors who are looking for reviews is on Facebook. I have listed a few of my favourite Groups and Pages in the Resources section. If you choose to go this way, it will definitely deliver a result for your book.

By the way, if you're ready to publish ten or twelve books each year, please get in touch with me by e-mail. I have an Inner Circle collaboration group, but it demands that you show up every month with a different book at 99c.

99c Promotions

It's true that Success Breeds Success, and 99c Promotions will all contribute to your book's popularity and have an effect on its Sales Ranking. Even an extra twenty sales in a short period can be enough to boost you from (say) 50,000 to top 20,000. Of course this is a temporary spike, but it's one more small thing on your Sales Page that will convince some casual browsers that your book is popular, and they will buy. If you can actively sustain 99c promotion, which does require you to make an effort over a week or two, you'll definitely see results.

There's a cumulative effect which will slope off much slower than a spike which only occurs in one day. A side-effect of interacting with other authors in this way is that you'll acquire additional Facebook Friends, and then you have a natural audience when it comes to more regular promotional postings on your Facebook Page. Of course you can expect to see a commensurate amount of reciprocal traffic, and it's important that you put in as much as you take out, but the general activity level will ensure that your profile goes up, and your sales will naturally follow.

You have to think strategically with promotions of any kind. It's not viable to keep your book on 99c promotion forever or you'll never make any money (you're only getting 35% at 99c). So you should plan ahead, pick (say) a four-week promotional period maybe a month or two after your book is launched, and run all your low-cost promotions within that period.

Keyword Bumps (Relevance)

Most Amazon customers use the default setting on their Search screen, which is 'Relevance'. We talked elsewhere about Keywords and their critical importance in your book's ranking. Whenever you promote your book within the wider community, you should always encourage your customers to use Keyword Search to find your book, instead of inserting the usual Amazon link. Each time someone searches on your chosen keyword and buys your book, it improves your 'Relevance' score in the Amazon algorithm, so your book will naturally rise in the ranking, irrespective of its actual sales rank in that keyword category. Again, you would be surprised about how effective keyword 'bumps' can be, especially if you are in small to medium-sized non-fiction niches. It also underlines the importance of including your major keyword phrases in your title and subtitle.

The lower in the rankings your book is, the more likely it is to benefit, and there's no easy way of calculating the viability of this scheme (unless you're an accomplished mathematician). However, you will soon know if your rankings improvement is driving a sales uplift. In my experience, you'll drive more buys-per-dollar using these methods than conventional advertising or shotgun Facebook posting.

Review Requests

We already talked about the importance of Reviews when you're trying to get momentum for your book, and Review Requests, working alongside the above two methods, are a good way to do this, as long as you stick to the rules.

Whereas your friends and relatives might be slow or even useless at reviewing your book, other authors know how to do it. It works particularly well for non-fiction, because the books are usually quick to read and the author-reader can easily form valid opinions about writing style, layout, content and formatting, which are the essential ingredients of a decent review. The other thing is that other Authors will rarely post a bad review. If they think your book needs work, they'll tell you privately, and they simply won't post a review at all.

You'll need to be equally active in your Author 'circle', so don't embark upon a promotion unless you are prepared to read a lot of books and invest some serious time in writing credible and honest appraisals. For me, I devote weekends to this activity. When I started, I was reviewing anyone who asked, but I soon realised that reviewing non-fiction books versus full-length novels meant that I simply didn't have time to read all the books I bought, so I wasn't doing justice to the Reviews. These days I only review non-fiction authors with books of a reasonable length, or shorter-novels (novellas). If I don't like the book, I'll message the author privately and let them know, usually making a suggestion that they should get their book edited and let me take another shot at it.

One benefit is that you'll learn a lot about how other authors structure and format their books, and you can often carry these lessons into your own publishing. I have also learned about subjects I didn't even know existed, and as a writer it's important to constantly broaden your horizons if you're to maintain a good pipeline of new ideas.

One particular benefit for UK authors promoting this way is that it's a great way to get Reviewed (and improve your Rankings) on Amazon.com in America. Likewise, US authors often struggle to get traction in the UK market, so you'll be popular with your new friends if you're a customer and reviewer on Amazon.co.uk.

To be clear: swapping *sales* is within the allowable tactics, that is to say that it does not breach Amazon's Terms of Service. Swapping *reviews* however is not, so be very careful. Amazon's response to blatant review swapping is usually to delete blocks of reviews without warning. One Author I know lost more than 500 reviews in one fell swoop recently, for precisely this reason.

One more point: if you download a book and review it, make sure that you read it, even if you speed-read or skim, past the 10% point in the book. The Amazon system is sophisticated, and each time your Kindle or iPad syncs with the bookstore, the reader data is uploaded from your device. So Amazon knows how much of the book you opened, and (anecdotally) how quickly you read it!

Don't cheat Amazon. It's your distributor, which also makes it your customer. Obviously there are endless opportunities to game the Amazon system, but the risk is that if you're caught, you may be banned from the platform.

E-Mail Marketing

I could (and probably will) write an entire book on e-mail marketing for Authors, so this is just a summary of why you should be doing it, and how to set about kicking it off.

Many of the gurus out there will talk about creating your 'Author Platform' in order to build a big audience for your books. I must confess that I ignored this when I first started, because I couldn't get any shape on it. But as time has gone on I have realised the value, and now I am an advocate, particularly of building e-mail lists.

E-mail marketing massively outstrips all social network and conventional advertising in terms of its effect on your book sales, but if you're starting from a zero base, you need to get working on it as soon as you can.

The central objective is to build a list (or lists) of people's e-mail addresses who have shown some interest in your work, so that you can launch new books and promote existing books directly to them. The hit rate, especially if you offer free or discounted books, can be staggeringly successful. There are lots of books out there, as well as online courses, blogs, etc., to tell you how to manage and exploit your e-mail list once you have a few dozen, hundred, or thousand names on there; typically Newsletters are the way to go, in order to connect people emotionally to your writing and books. This is for a future book, but in order to get you started, here's how I do it;

Create an Offer

You need a reason for people to join your list. This should be something of value that you can offer for free, in order to get people to click on a link in your book. Internet Marketers will use this click to start a *Sales Funnel*, which pours lots of people in the top, and ends with a series of product sales of increasing value as they descend through the stages of the process. That's great if you have the services or *upsell products*, such as audio products, coaching courses, or similar add-ons for your business. However, if you're an Author without any upsell, you are simply trying to build a list so that you can launch and promote your new books when you're ready.

As you work your way through this book, you might come across a link or two for some of my free products. In particular, I use what I call *Missing Chapter* mini-books of around 3000 words on a specific subject. The one you'll find in here is a small book called *"How to Use Stunning Covers to Sell More Books"*. I wrote it in a day, and it includes step-by-step tuition about how to build a Book Cover using Microsoft Publisher, a simple but effective software package that most people have access to, and which is much simpler and cheaper than Photoshop, which most people screw up! I have padded the book with lots of screen shots to walk them through the process, so the 3000 words ends up at around 45 pages, adding perceived value to the free product. It's a useful little book and it teaches something potentially very valuable, given the cost of buying covers from outside.

Stunning Covers is stored as a PDF file on the Public section of my Dropbox account, so anyone who has the link can download it directly to their PC or Tablet and read it or print it out. It also contains more promotional links to my other books, so it acts as a link in a chain to get people to come back to Amazon and explore my other work, in particular my book *"Mile High Word Count and Writing Productivity"* which is the sequel to this book. It also works the other way, because if they buy that book, the *Stunning Covers* offer is in there, and leads them eventually to this book on Amazon. I hope you're beginning to see how these things all link together.

So, how do I get their e-mail address?

I use a subscription service called AWeber (http://www.aweber.com), which allows me to set up mailing lists, and then build registration forms (sometimes called *squeeze pages)*, which I can easily embed in the code of a page on one of my websites. The link I put in my book leads to this form on the website. The process works like this:

o The reader clicks on the hyperlink in my book.

o Their Browser opens and launches the Squeeze Page on my Website.

o The form says something like *"Please register here to receive your Free copy of Stunning Covers and to receive my monthly newsletter"*

o Once they leave their details (just their name and e-mail address) they are added to the specific list at AWeber which is associated with that form (you can run infinite numbers of lists and forms)

o AWeber sends them an 'Opt-In' e-mail, in order to confirm that it's their real address.

o They click once on this e-mail and AWeber sends a second e-mail (which I have designed) that includes a welcome message and the direct link to the Dropbox server where they can download *Stunning Covers.*

So, they have the free book, and I have their e-mail address. But, more importantly, they *know* that they have subscribed to my newsletter, so when they receive it a few days or weeks later, they're not surprised or offended that I have e-mailed them. The set-up took less than one hour. Believe me when I say I am *not* an IT geek in any way, shape, or form!

From there onwards, it's about e-mail marketing, which is an entirely different dark art!

I'm sure that if you have a couple of glasses of Pinot, you'll soon come up with an idea for a Free Product that you can use in this way. And you don't have to pay for AWeber if you're on a tight budget: you can use Mail Chimp, which does the same thing for free until you hit 2000 people on your list. The more compelling your offer, the higher the rate that people will click through and sign up.

Most importantly, you need to get this going quickly, because every reader that doesn't have the chance to join your list is one you'll never get back. I only realised this after I'd had over 8000 downloads for my *Master Self-Hypnosis in a Weekend* recorded scripts, and I hadn't captured a single one. As soon as I understood it, I fixed it. That list is now growing at over 300 names a month, and every one of them is interested in Self Hypnosis, so you can guess what I'll be mailing them about in the future!

A secondary source of e-mail addresses, which is even better *qualified*, comes from the simple action of including my e-mail address in the front and back of *this* book. The Author community is so curious and eager for knowledge that I get at least ten e-mails a week from readers who either have a question, some typos to report, or are asking me to read and review their book. I always answer within 24 hours and try to help wherever I can. It's worth it, because again I have captured another ten e-mail addresses, from people who have taken the time to contact me. Of course, I know what they're interested in, so guess who'll be the first folks to get an e-mail from me when this new edition is launched!

Mark my words; if there's one thing I'd do differently if I was starting again in the Self-Publishing game, it would be to devote some time and energy to putting my e-mail list-building in place from day one. It's simple, it's cheap (even free) and it gives you the most powerful promotional asset that *money can't buy*; an audience to launch your next book to!

By the way, if you want to see how this works, here's the link. Just click on it, and you'll see the various stages play out on your screen. Plus, you'll have your own copy of *"How to Use Stunning Covers to Sell More Books",* and you'll receive my Newsletter every so often!

http://tiny.cc/a232gx

13 – Marketing Inside Amazon

Since the First Edition of this book was published in October 2013, Amazon has launched a series of significant Marketing programs for its Authors to leverage, some of which have been mentioned in earlier sections. Let's take a look at these programs in more detail.

Kindle Unlimited

Kindle Unlimited (KU) is Amazon's *all you can eat* subscription program, which arrived in the USA in the Summer of 2014, and has been subsequently extended to the UK. The basic features of the program are as follows;

- KU subscribers can download and read unlimited books from the Amazon Kindle store, for a subscription of $9.95 a month. The subscription rate for UK had not been announced at time of publication, but is expected to be in the range of £5.95-£6.95. Subscribers can have up to ten books at any one time on their device, and once they hit this threshold, they must delete titles in order to download new ones. Unlike KOLL (Kindle Owners Lending Library) that allowed one free book per month for Amazon Prime members (which would be deleted automatically after 30 days), KU books do not time-out.

- Not all books on the Kindle store are enrolled in KU. For independent Authors, your book is automatically included in KU when you enrol in KDP Select. If you're not in KDP Select, you can't participate in KU. Many of the major publishing houses have opted out of KU (for obvious reasons), however for those that have opted in, the deal is different for their books, so for the purpose of this explanation we'll ignore them. At time of writing, around 650,000 books are included in the KU library.

- Any customer in the USA or UK clicking through to a KU-enrolled book's Sales Page will see the option to *Read it Free with Kindle Unlimited*. As you can imagine, the decision criteria to download it, using the usual One Click button, is completely different from having to pay for it, so it has the potential (and indeed has proved to be) a major disrupter to the usual consumer behaviour. Later in this section we will examine ways in which you, the independent self-publisher, can leverage this to your advantage.

- Amazon qualifies a KU-downloaded book for royalty payment only when the book has been read (opened) past its 10% point. If the book isn't read that far, the author will not receive any payment, although the download may still show up in the 'Orders' graph on the first page of the KDP Reports dashboard.

- Amazon has been a little sketchy over some of the finer details, in particular whether a KU download has parity with a normal sale when it comes to Rankings, however the consensus at time of writing is that there is no difference. I will update this chapter, and issue a bulletin on my websites www.ricksmithbooks and www.spmasterclass.com if and when different information is made public.

- Qualifying KU downloads earn the same royalty as a book borrowed under KOLL. This is based on a share of the *global fund* and it varies from month to month. We'll examine this in more detail shortly, because it may become a major factor in your decision to stay in or opt out of the program (and KDP Select entirely) in the future.

Given the explosive success of other *all you can eat* content programs, such as Netflix, Amazon Prime Video, LastFM, and Spotify, Kindle Unlimited was probably inevitable. In common with these programs, it's far from universally popular amongst content creators, in this case *You the Independent Author*. Of course it's early days, and it's clear from the vagueness of Amazon's pitch to us that the program is still in *beta* until they assemble enough data to make solid judgements about its success, its impact on their retail e-book business, and its take-up by readers and authors alike.

Most important (in my personal opinion) is that we, the Author Community, keep an open mind until we see what the longer-term effect is. There's a trade-off here. Amazon needs to ensure that they keep the program sufficiently lucrative for Authors and Publishers, so that we don't start opting out, thereby limiting the amount of product available to Subscribers. As one might expect in the first couple of months, Amazon are squeezing the royalty rates downward until they hear the pips squeak. From a high of more than $2.00 per download under KOLL alone in June 2014, a rate of $1.54 occurred in August. Again, I'll update this info as it happens, but if it falls any further I suspect there will be an exodus.

In terms of pure earnings, at $2.00 royalty a $2.99 book would earn more or less the same for a sale versus a KU or KOLL download. As it's impossible to earn the 70% rate if your book is priced lower, Amazon has the upper hand in the short-term.

A number of interesting dynamics have occurred since KU was launched. Based on my own catalog, which comprises 'serious books for grown-ups' and 'fun books for kids and young adults' the following changes occurred:

1. The serious books (priced between $4 and $5) have been boosted by KU. Sales have *continued* along their usual trajectory, but KOLL/KU downloads *increased* by around 150% on average. So the effect of KU has been incremental. I like that a lot, especially as it's likely that some of the 'borrows' actually turn into sales later, as is the case with books like this, where people use them as guide books for the long-term.

2. The kids' books ($2.99) have shown a completely different pattern. Sales have *decreased* by around 35%, whereas KOLL/KU downloads have *increased* by almost 400% on average. The net result is that these books are now moving significantly more units as KU downloads than actual sales. I would also add that these books sell significantly more in paperback than e-book, and these sales have not been affected in the slightest. Overall revenue from these books is up, obviously as a result of Kindle Unlimited.

So it looks like the kids, who have a limited budget but consume genre and series books voraciously, are net beneficiaries of Kindle Unlimited. This in turn offers a clue as to where Authors should be focusing their future efforts if they want to take advantage of the KU deal. Working with Amazon is about being adaptable, as the various programs are constantly changing and evolving.

Of course, as these kids' books are priced at $2.99, the payout for KU was initially similar to the royalty on a straight sale. But as the monthly payout decreases, this is no longer so attractive for the author. At $2.00 versus $1.50, given the increase in volume, it's heading towards a zero sum. We could continue with the statistical analysis, however right now it's fairly clear what is happening, and we need to see what Amazon do with the payout rates over the coming months.

Another factor is that the first month of KU is a free-trial period, which also skews the numbers. In the first month in the USA there was massive take-up, but from the data it's clear that some of those early trialists chose not to move on to the paid program once their 30 day trial ended, and the borrow rates for the kids books declined by around 30% in month two. However, it's reasonable to assume that this is a short-term effect, and that KU will steadily build it's subscriber base over time. Ideally, we need to see twelve months of data in order to spot the trends and patterns, so that will ensure that the Third Edition of this book has something new to report next year!

So, if we accept that KU is here to stay, and probably precipitating a major shift in e-book buying habits, how should the independent author adapt to take advantage of it?

Well, you could leave your head in the sand and hope for the best; it's probable that your income will decline steadily as more people move onto the KU deal and stop buying books outright.

Alternately, if you understand what drives a typical KU customer, you could tailor your approach to take maximum advantage of the fact that the tipping point for downloading your book has dramatically shifted to the left. Of course, the world of internet marketers, crap authors, and outsourcers will jump on this bandwagon and ramp up their output of thirty page pamphlets on how to tie your shoe-laces, and no doubt some of them will make a few bucks along the way. They are your real competition, and if you know how to get better visibility for your quality output, you should have no problem beating them off.

So, if you're willing to think and work in a different way, or even to develop a separate catalog of books specifically targeted for KU readers, there's a huge opportunity here, particularly for non-fiction authors.

Write shorter books

Obviously, if you're going to earn less per book, you need to make time to generate more books in order to grow your income. That means you probably can't afford to spend weeks or months writing (and revising) 300-page books like this one. A book like this could easily be broken down into three shorter 100-page books, targeted specifically at KU subscribers. If all three sections were downloaded separately on KU, the Author payout across the three titles would be significantly more than the royalty on a single sale of the larger book.

Raise your Price

It's always been the case that higher-priced books attracted more 'borrows' under the old KOLL program. The dynamic here is *perceived value*. Think about it; if you see something you'd like to read, and it's priced at (say) $5.99, you'll definitely like the idea of 'putting one over' on the system by getting it for free! This is meat and drink for KU.

Of course none of these tactics are going to work unless you concentrate on the perceived value and perceived quality of your books, so...

Work on your Brand and Catalog

If you can entice a KU subscriber to download and read one of your books, it shouldn't be too much trouble to get them to read your other titles, especially if they're related. For this to work, you need to make "Brand Author" notable, or they won't have a common thread to lead them from one book to the next. Here, I have a couple of suggestions:

Your Author Name; if you have a complicated, double barrelled, or hard-to-pronounce name, *change it*. Either drop part of it, or get a pen name. I'm very lucky that my name (Rick Smith) is not only my real name, but also really short and easy to remember. What's more, I can print it on my covers in much larger type than a longer name, so my books are easier to spot on the Search page than if my name was unreadable on a thumbnail sized-cover. Trust me, nobody gives a rat's ass what you're called; this is simply a device to make you more discoverable and memorable.

I have used pen names, and my most successful one is *Joey K*, which was designed to meet the same criteria.

Consistency of Style; Your objective is to get people to read *all* your books, so not only developing a consistent style for your covers, but also the way that you hook readers with your *Look Inside* section is important too.

Here's what you want people to think to themselves: *"I like this author because I always know what I'm getting!"*

Concentrate on Stunning Covers

More than ever before, a crappy cover is gong to hurt you. The aforementioned get-rich-quick outsourcers know this, because that's how they often trick potential customers into clicking on their shitty books in the first place. Under KU, people may not even bother to read the *Look Inside* section on your Sales Page at all: why bother?

So, however you choose to approach this new landscape, you should raise your game if you haven't been too fussed about cover design in the past. Packaging and presentation will be key differentiators in the new world of KU. Of course it goes without saying that if you follow the advice in the earlier sections, your content will be of a much higher standard than the scalpers who get their $20 manuscripts from freelancers in Bangladesh.

Adapt your Product Descriptions

Another feature of your Sales Page which is going to be much more important in the future is your Product Description. This is the place where the typical Amazon customer will make up their mind if you're serious. How many times do you browse for a book, and the first line of the Product Description says something like:

"Get this Amazon Best-Seller TODAY ONLY for 99c. Usual Price $4.99"

Don't do it. It's a cheap, tacky, Internet-Marketer tactic, which has totally lost its value in the modern age. Just because you're publishing shorter books, that's no reason to drop your standards. Write your Product Description like your book is selling at ten bucks. You know what your marketing strategy is about, but your customer is always looking for top quality content at the lowest (in this case 'free') price. Keep the bar high, and let the rip-off merchants come up to your level, rather than dropping down to theirs.

You're in this for the long-haul, and over time your quality will always be the biggest determining factor in your success. Above all, don't panic. KU might be important, but you still need to offer commensurate quality to your readers who want to actually buy your book.

Think Differently About your First 10%

If you've understood the earlier section on *Look Inside*, you can probably imagine that it's even more important now. Firstly, you have to get people to read *past* 10% if you're going to qualify for a payout from Amazon, so you need to ensure that you give away only as much as you need to, in order to hook people in to reading beyond that point. But in the same breath, you need to make sure that the quality of the writing us up to scratch, so that they don't abandon your book before they hit that milestone. Remember, it's notionally free to the reader, so if you fail to capture their imagination in the first 10%, they'll dump your book and move onto something else, leaving you penniless.

10% of a (say) 70-page book really isn't much at all. So get rid of any superfluous front matter, shorten your copyright statements, dump any dedications, links, or offers to the back of the book, and make sure you get down to business really quick. If they can't get a flavor for your content from *Look Inside*, you've lost the sale (download) before you've even begun. Keep your focus; your sole objective is to get them to download and read past 10%. All the other important stuff (like reviews) comes later.

I would also recommend that if you decide to design books for the KU target market, you stop using headings like Preface, Introduction, and About the Author. This is a completely different buyer's behavior from that of a book that you're trying to sell for big money. Minimize distraction, get straight to the point, and convince your potential reader that you're delivering quality material, quickly.

I can already hear the fiction authors complaining that much of this doesn't help them. Sorry, but you guys have to tailor these recommendations to your style and content accordingly. I don't think there's that much difference in how you hook a reader in either fiction or non-fiction. The objectives are the same: *download my book and read it past 10% so I can get paid!*

There are no experts in Kindle Unlimited, because it hasn't been around long enough. But if you apply these recommendations, as I will be doing for the next year or two, you should at least be ahead of the majority of Authors, who haven't got a clue what to do! KU is here to stay, and you can either show up and play, or go home and starve!

Kindle Countdown Deals

Kindle Countdown Deals, a new promotional program launched by Amazon in the Spring of 2014, has proved to be highly successful for many Independent Authors. As I have not yet used it for any of my books, I asked my friend and fellow Independent Author Glen Ford to write a section based on his experience with the Countdown Program. This is what Glen has to say...

Kindle Countdown

There are only two reasons that you might want to use free as a price point. The first is that you are using the so-called *freemium* to drive sales to a more expensive product. That is the technique suggested by most internet marketers. The second is that you are using the loss-leader product to develop a market that will pay for itself at a later date, typically with some form of on-going charge. This technique has been used quite successfully in areas as diverse as film cameras and internet search.

From a writer's point of view, there are three major problems with using free as a promotional tool. These problems apply whether you are using the Kindle Free Promotions that are available through KDP Select, or if you are using a *permafree* solution.

The first is that most of the people who are going to download free books aren't particularly interested in your book. In fact, most of them will never read your book. They won't see what a wonderfully thoughtful and capable writer you are. Therefore, they won't be motivated to buy your other books. For a writer, the whole point of providing free is to sell your other books. And unfortunately, free just doesn't work very well for that purpose.

The second is that you have given a copy to people who might have been interested in paying for your book. In essence, you've just undercut and eliminated the market for your book. And you've just devalued your book. After all, why should people pay for something that they can get free?

The third problem is that you haven't been paid for your book. All the work you've put into your book should and must produce a return for you. And of course, free books don't produce revenue. While this may be acceptable if the item is producing indirect revenue, when coupled with the other problems you can see that free just isn't that effective for books as a revenue generator.

From Amazon's point of view, there are three big problems with free.

Firstly, it costs them the same as if they had sold the book. Yet it doesn't produce a direct return for them. This was fine while they were developing the market for eBooks. But as the book market switched from paper to electronic, a point was reached where the benefits of providing free books was less than the costs. This is especially true for permanently free books.

Secondly, a large number of books have been set to permanently free. Generally, this is done by publishing them on alternative sites such as Smashwords. These sites allow free books. The publisher then arranges for Amazon to competitively match those prices. Frequently, this is done by internet marketers who are using Amazon as an advertising media to sell other products. Unfortunately, these books are often of low quality and are worth exactly what is being spent for them.

Finally, Amazon is a merchandising company first and foremost. They know that too frequent promotions will backfire. Effectively if a price is cut more than once in 60 to 90 days then readers will devalue the book to the promotion price.

Given the rather senseless abuse of free books by internet marketers, and the cost to Amazon, it was inevitable that Amazon would begin to back away from supporting free books. There are several indications that they have begun to do so. Amazon no longer counts free books towards the all-important sales ranking. They have introduced two "free" book programs (Prime and Unlimited), which are actually paid memberships. And they have introduced a new promotional tool called Kindle Countdown.

So what is Kindle Countdown?

Kindle countdown is Amazon's method of overcoming the problems inherent with promoting free books. In more generic terms, a countdown sale is a form of time-limited sale. The price is dropped for a specific period only. At the end of that time, the price returns to the regular selling price. Typically, the sale is stepped through a series of prices. For example, it may be 90% off for 2 days, then 50% off for 2 more and then 25% off for 2 more. As an incentive, the remaining period is normally displayed. This display of time remaining is an important motivator to purchasers as they are afraid to miss the special price. You've seen this same technique used every time you've seen a July sale or Sale with a visible end date.

Kindle's countdown sale works the same way as these more generic countdown sales. You as the Publisher decide to run a Countdown sale. The sale starts on a specific date and time and runs to a specific date and time. You choose the lowest price in steps of one dollar or one pound from 99 (cents or pence). You are then given a choice of the number of one dollar or one pound steps the book can go through. Based on that choice, a recommended date and time to move to the following price steps are provided. You can accept the recommendation or adjust them. Once the sale initiates, the price will change at the selected date and time. The original price, the sale price and the time remaining will all show on the product's page. These two elements help to spur purchasers to complete the sale.

Any sales that occur use the same royalty calculation as you earn with regular prices. So 99-cent sales can earn you up to 69 cents per book rather than the 35 cents that is normal for that price point. However, be warned that the delivery cost is not adjusted. Your sale price must consider delivery costs. If you have an expensive eBook, you could easily find every sale losing you money!

Kindle's Countdown sale program does have several limitations. Generally, speaking these limits are imposed in order to avoid issues with customer opinion as well as legal issues. The limitations are:

o One sale per book in each territory of up to 5 days in a 90-day period

o A Countdown promotion prevents using the free promotion

o The product price must not have been changed during the 30 days prior to the sale

o Products must be available for 30 days prior to the sale

o The product price must not change during the 30 days following the sale

o Minimum price is 99 cents or 99 pence.

o Price increases are $1.00 (or £1.00) only.

o Maximum of five price increases (one per day) or less.

o You may not adjust the sale within one day of its start. Nor may you close the sale.

There are several advantages to using the Kindle countdown sale. The biggest is the fact that the issues associated with free promotions are avoided. Amazon counts all sales towards your sales rank. The value of the book is not adversely affected by the sale (as it may be by free promotions). You are not damaging your market (the 90 day rule largely prevents that). And you are earning money directly from your sales. It may not be as much as it would be, but your sales will also be much higher.

In addition to that, Amazon does promote your books under Countdown. A heading on the main categories page lists all the books under Countdown deals. Unlike the other book deals, if your book is on Countdown it will automatically show in the list. This does not imply your book won't need other promotion, but it does give you a leg up on Amazon's site.

The biggest downsides are related to Amazon's partial implementation of the Countdown. Only the U.S. and U.K. are able to participate at the moment. That means when you sell books through this program, you have eliminated your ability to promote books in countries such as Canada, Australia, India, Japan and the European Union. If you are a typical independent publisher, this can have a significant effect on your overall sales.

In addition, while book prices are set based on the exchange rate difference between the U.S. and the U.K., the countdown sale prices are not. While prices start at 99 cents in the U.S., they also start at 99 pence in the U.K. or roughly $1.60 U.S.. Then they increase the price in $1.60 steps. A typical $2.99 book in the U.S. would have two steps, one at 67% off and one at 33% off. The same book in the U.K. would normally cost £1.76 and only have one step at £0.99 or 56% off. The deal is just not good enough to start U.K. readers buying.

Finally, many of your typical promotional outlets will not accept Kindle countdown sales. This is not universally true, as some have created specific sites for 99-cent sales. However, many of the most effective no longer accept countdown sales listings.

To get the most out of the Kindle countdown sale you need to do certain things and have certain conditions present:

o   Kindle countdown sales work best the higher the initial price of your book. An $8.99 book is more likely to become a best seller at 99 cents than a $2.99 book will.

o   You will be eliminating promotions to countries other than the U.S. and the U.K. so it is most suitable for books that do not sell well in other countries. In fact, the promotion really works well only for the U.S. so even U.K. sales should be considered as dispensable.

o   You will need to have a separate list of promotion sites from your free promotion sites. While some sites will continue to list your book, many will not. Those that do will have a radically different click through rate.

You will need to have a separate launch strategy from free books. Typically, free days are used to gain reviews for new books. That isn't possible if you are intending to use countdown sales during the first 90 days. One technique I have used successfully is to launch using a reduced price and using the free promotions for the first 90 days. My last free promotion then states that this is the last time the book will be free. Another technique I've used is to reduce my price for 30 days, return to the regular price, and then do a countdown sale during the final 30 days. At this point, I have not noticed a major difference in the results between the two methods.

Glen Ford is a prolific Independent Author, Publisher, Project Manager, Training Consultant and all-round good guy. Here are his contact details;

http://www.glendford.com - personal site, project management, & business management topics

http://www.learningcreators.com - how to create learning (one on one training, courseware, and how to books) http://www.trainingnow.ca - publisher of training courses and books

https://www.facebook.com/glen.ford.739 - Facebook account (will friend almost anyone) https://www.facebook.com/Glen.D.Ford.PMP - Facebook page (likes)

http://www.amazon.com/author/glendford - Amazon page (main, business/writing/project management)

http://amzn.com/e/B007DZTTRU - Amazon page (Glen Douglas - gardening primarily)

Amazon Pre-Orders

Another recent addition to the Amazon marketing arsenal for Authors is Pre-Orders. Of course this isn't really new; it's been available to the mainstream Publishing houses forever. But Amazon has now extended it so that anyone on the platform can use it. Here's how it works, and why it's useful;

You can make your new books available for pre-order in Kindle Stores worldwide. Setting a pre-order allows customers to order your book as early as 90 days before it's release date.

One advantage of pre-order is that you can start promoting your book in advance, to build up some demand and interest. You can promote your book on Author Central, Goodreads, your website, and anywhere else you like. Any pre-orders you get will count toward your Sales Rank before your book is even released.

You'll list your book as you would with any other KDP book. When you're adding a new book, on Step 4 of the KDP dashboard *Select Your Book Release Option,* select *"Make my book available for pre-order"* and set a future publication date. Amazon will set up a Sales page in exactly the same format as if you had already launched it, except there won't be a *Look Inside* or *Download a Sample* function, so you'll need to be very precise with your Product Description.

Customers can order the book anytime leading up to the release date, and it will be delivered to them on that date. You can list pre-orders books in all Amazon international marketplaces except India. On publication day, your book will become available at midnight in each marketplace.

When you list a book for pre-order, you'll need to upload the final version *or a draft manuscript* of the book file for review. You'll have a chance to update the manuscript to the final version up to ten days in advance of the publication date. Your final manuscript *must* be uploaded at least ten days before the release date you set. This time-line is anecdotally flexible, but never in your favor, so be very careful if you decide to use Pre-Orders for your book. If you miss the deadline for uploading the final version of your manuscript, Amazon will unceremoniously ban you from using the Pre-Order program for a year, and they don't negotiate!

14 – Getting Great Reviews

Introduction

If you owned an internet sales business (maybe you do) you would probably pay close attention to the quality of the products you sell, because that would be an important factor in your success or failure. However, because Amazon has thrown open its sales platform to anyone who has something to sell, it's impossible for them to quality control all the products passing through their ecosystem, especially when it comes to books. Frankly, there is some utter dross on the Kindle Bookstore, and occasionally you may get suckered into buying and downloading a real turkey.

So Amazon's way of dealing with the quality control aspects for Kindle (and physical) books, is to let the market self-regulate, and that happens through the Review System. If you know all about the Review format, you might skip ahead, but if you've never encountered it before, here's how it works and how important it is to respect it when it comes to your book(s).

Anyone can review any product on Amazon, and the *moderation filters*, that is to say the rules for allowing or blocking a review, are quite loose. Just like the Sales Ranking system, there's a ranking algorithm built into the Review system, which is much more sophisticated than it appears. Each review earns between one and five stars, and after a few reviews have been acquired, the average review is shown up-top next to the Book Title, so that people can instantly scan to see the apparent quality of the book. Opinion is divided about the relevance of Reviews on your Sales Ranking. But what's for sure is that having no reviews at all will ensure you're book languishes precisely nowhere in any kind of ranking at all.

The Amazon review system is smart enough to pick up on some popular scams, such as the same people constantly giving five star reviews to the same authors, and even (anecdotally) a pass/fail check on reviews which come from Amazon account holders whose physical address is the same as the author (such as a wife reviewing her husband's book, even if she legitimately bought and read it). Nevertheless, there are gaps in the system, and if you search around to find the highest ranked Reviewers, some of them don't even post real language in their reviews, just character groups or gobbledegook. I cannot adequately express how angry I get when I see this kind of thing!

Amazon Verified Purchase

Any review you acquire is valid, but the most valuable are 'Amazon Verified Purchase' reviews, which are posted by people who actually bought the product. I can read your thoughts here, so bear in mind that there are experts who say that the review System even knows if someone buys a product and has had long enough to actually read it before they post the review! Anyway, just like Sales Rankings and Search Engines, there's Dark Art in play, to prevent people from gaming the system too much. Reviews are very important, both *artistically*, to persuade browsers that your book is worthy of their money, and *technically*, for raising you up the Rankings ladder, so it is to be respected and handled with care.

If you write a good book, and people like it, you will get good reviews and these will help you on many levels to become more successful. If you write a bad book, especially if it's perceived as poor value, the Reviewers will hammer you, and you'll be out of business. If you meet some peoples' expectations but not others, you may get a few poor reviews, but this is part of being in the creative business, so suck it up and move on. Whatever you do, never try to engage directly with a Reviewer, even if they cane you. If a Review is grossly unfair or seriously offensive, you can ask Amazon Customer Services to investigate and take it down, in which case the Reviewer may have their account blocked, so flame wars rarely happen on Amazon Reviews.

Reviews can also be a really entertaining place to drift for a little while when you're looking for inspiration. If you want a solid belly laugh which will really cheer you up, go look at the reviews for "Veet for Men Hair Removal Cream" and you'll see what I mean. Seriously, it's one of the funniest things you'll ever come across on the Internet, and has become something of a *cause celebre* for Amazon Reviewers.

Why Reviews Are Important To You

Reviews lend credibility to your book, and tell prospective purchasers what other people thought about it. Remember the 'Wisdom of Crowds' mantra that crops up time and time again? Once they are in their chosen search category, people will rely on others' experiences to tell them if your book is worthwhile. Once they're reading your reviews, most of them have made a purchasing commitment to buy a book on the subject, and the quality of your reviews will exert serious influence towards whether they buy yours. Review quality is up there with the quality of your Product Description as a key decision factor for your customers, so you need to focus on getting some good ones.

Dealing with Bad Reviews

As regards bad reviews, here's a paradox. A "bad bad" review, written poorly by someone who was obviously grumpy or made a bad decision, will stand out to most buyers as just that, *buyer's remorse*, and you won't lose points for having one or two of those.

I recently received a bad review for my 'Learning Masonic Ritual' book, which is a long-time category bestseller, which didn't make any sense to me. The reviewer seemed to be thoroughly pissed that I hadn't revealed the secrets of Freemasonry, which was absolutely not the point of the book (the clue is in the title). So I clicked through to look at his other reviews and from what I could see I deduced that he was (is) a New Age Conspiracy Theorist, and had bought my book for completely the wrong reason. So his review was actually a rant at himself for not having read the blurb properly, and definitely not having read the *Look Inside* section, or he would have been completely clear on the purpose of this book. So I stopped worrying about how his negativity might affect my sales, and realised that anyone in this niche category reading his review would work out for themselves that it was irrelevant!

More dangerous is a "good bad" review, that is to say one which takes you apart using good grammar and solid reasoning. This is not about someone saying they didn't enjoy your book, though that's bad enough. This is when someone critiques your content, your characters, or your writing style, seriously. If you get one or two of these, you need to think carefully about whether there's something wrong with your book, correct it, and maybe re-launch under a different title and author name!

Most people will only write a seriously bad review about your book if they feel really strongly about it. I often get the odd *"didn't learn what I wanted"'* on my How-To books, but rarely less than three stars. If you start getting reviews that criticise your grammar, layout, spelling or other controllable and correctable errors in your manuscript, you need to hire an editor and get a corrected version up as soon as possible. Critique for these things means you've been careless or sloppy, and that's unforgiveable if you're serious about making money as a writer. Hopefully that can't happen to you because you've worked through the step-by-step processes in Section 2 before you uploaded your book,

Another reason why Reviews are critical is because they are an important component of your search visibility. The balance between quality and quantity of reviews is unclear, but you can be sure that your average star rating is pretty important. There are other factors, like whether many people have clicked on the *'I found this review useful'* button, which also has the effect of raising popular reviews up the list and dropping unpopular ones down until they may eventually disappear completely.

In the medium-sized niches that most non-fiction authors write for, just six or seven decent reviews will be enough to populate your Sales Page. Reviews are equally as important for Fiction as Non-Fiction, except that a money-making fiction title may need upwards of fifty or sixty reviews before it's making the royalties commensurate with the effort expended. Fiction genres are generally much more competitive than non-fiction, and the commitment to read and review a fiction book might run into days, rather than hours for non-fiction.

Based on my own experiences, around fifty good (five and four-star) reviews will provide tremendous support for your book in Search, and ensure it stays in the top few rows, even if sales fluctuate. For this reason alone, it's well worth the effort of hustling for as many reviews as you can get, from wherever you can legitimately obtain them. Ten in the first month, and fifty in the first year, are good targets to aim for.

Getting Your First Reviews

The blogosphere is full of debate about what is considered ethical or unethical about getting reviews for a newly launched book. I deliberately stay out of the debate because I believe that quality will ultimately shine through. As Barack Obama famously said, *"You can put lipstick on a pig, (but) it's still a pig"*.

If your book is good, and you get a little help to bring it to the attention of an appreciative public, you may simply be levelling the field against the marketing muscle of the big publishers, as long as no laws are broken and the spirit of fair play isn't violated. Some say that asking friends to buy your book and review it is a perfectly reasonable tactic, as long as you don't influence or coerce them into stating anything in the review that is knowingly false or misleading. You should not write reviews for your own book, of course.

Stick to the Rules

Amazon has rules (the Terms of Service, or TOS), and these are constantly changing so you should familiarise yourself with the latest version through the Kindle or CreateSpace websites.

I recommend you stay within ethical boundaries by informing everyone you know (and I do mean everyone) that you have a book out and that you'd be very grateful if they'd consider buying it, reading it, and reviewing it. In the Pricing section we talked about launching at 99c/99p for the first few weeks, and if you have friends who aren't willing to spend 99c to get your masterpiece, then I think you should get some new friends! By the way, just asking once will not do the job. You need to make a nuisance of yourself for a few weeks. Inertia will otherwise prevail, but if you keep on at them, in the end you'll embarrass them (in a nice way) to read your book and post the Review!

Facebook is a great way to keep yourself up in their front-of mind, but be assured that it will only serve you well for your friends. Strangers will rarely respond to this kind of proposal or pressure, and you'll burn a lot of engine hours trying to market yourself to the world, with not much return on investment.

Remember, in the launch phase, you're trying to get maybe six or seven decent reviews, so focus on who and where those are going to come from, and make sure you get them whilst your book is still in its 99c launch promotional period. Once it takes off, which hopefully it will, you will be lucky to get 1% of the general buying public to review you, so these early reviews are the bedrock of your Sales Page, and you should cultivate and curate them carefully.

Multi-Country Reviews

If you're launching your book on Amazon.com (for the USA, South Africa etc.) bear in mind that these reviews will not normally show up on Amazon in the UK. Likewise, Reviews you get from amazon.co.uk won't populate on the US Sales Page. They are sometimes visible as a click-through, but you ideally need to get some Reviews from both populations. As you've learned, there are some good Writers Groups on Facebook where other authors legitimately buy and review each other's books, and this can be very useful at the beginning, especially as you are likely to get well-considered and honest reviews from other authors. This is just a hi-tech version of 'Book Clubs' which are one of the key sources for major publishers' reviews. Again, you're levelling the field.

It is perfectly possible to post reviews for a book on multiple Amazon sites, however the important *'Amazon Verified Purchase'* will only appear on the site where you purchased the book. So if you buy a book from the UK site, then review it on both Amazon.co.uk and Amazon.com, the *verified* badge will only show up on the .uk site.

Most serious reviewers will usually copy/paste the review they post on their local Amazon site to the other big one(s). Think of it like this: if *you* wrote an honest review about a book you'd enjoyed (or otherwise), you'd want the whole world to hear what you have to say. So don't be afraid to ask a reviewer that you know, either personally or through Facebook, to make sure the review is posted on (at least) amazon.com and amazon.co.uk. The other international sites display a mix of reviews from *.com* and *.co.uk*, until they have a sufficient number of local reviews to populate the page.

Good and Bad Practice

Whatever you do, don't buy reviews online, from places like fiverr.com (although there are other excellent author services available there). You'll almost certainly be voiding Amazons rules, and if they get a sniff of something untoward, you could find all your reviews deleted and even your book suspended from sale.

You should most definitely be asking your readers to review your book by placing requests in the front and back matter of your manuscript, on your website or blog (if you have one) and anywhere else that's appropriate.

Once you gain some momentum, and your book starts to sell under its own steam, you will pick up natural reviews, and the better and more life-changing your book, the more people will be inspired to review you. If you should be fortunate enough to get 'real' reviews, based on books you send out to magazines or media outlets, make sure you get the reviewer to post on Amazon, or get their permission to place the review in your Product Description.

Hang out in Groups and Pages where you think your book buyers are congregating, and post some interesting stuff from time to time, so that people start looking forward to reading your posts. I have a Facebook Author friend, who lives in London too, but whom I have never met, who rarely posts on Facebook, except for first thing every Friday morning with a hilarious and uplifting 100-word Good Morning message to the world. Dozens of people comment on it every week, and it's universally anticipated. It's always the first thing I see in my Newsfeed when I sit down in my office, so he's timing it perfectly. It's brilliant; and it's just one of the simple little things that you can do. You don't need a complicated social media strategy to get a little following. If he asked me, I would instantly buy and review his new book, because he's cheered me up every Friday for the last few months!

In general, you can never have too many reviews (as long as they are good ones) so make a structured plan as soon as you're ready to launch your book, and don't stop promoting and pushing until you've got your five to seven reviews on each major Amazon Sales Page.

There's a list of writers' Facebook groups in the Resources section at the end, and some of the better ones are well organized to help you get the reviews you need, by legitimate means.

Press Reviews

Most of your Marketing effort should be directed inside the Amazon eco-system, because it's a complete world where you can promote and market to a captive population of buyers. It's responsive, so you get immediate feedback on whether your product and marketing are working, and it's essentially free if you use it wisely.

However, if you are ambitious about getting your book out to a wider audience, you may consider shooting for some press reviews.

The simple steps for this are:

Identify Relevant Publications, such as:

- Niche magazines

- Local Papers

- National and Regional Literary Supplements

- Book Clubs (online)

- Bloggers in your Sector

Contact Them Directly, either by e-mail or telephone, and identify the person who you should be targeting. It's pointless to simply send a copy of your book to a press outlet in the hope that it will find its way to the Reviewer; it won't. A simple phone call to the front desk should enable you to find out who handles book reviews and their e-mail address.

E-mail the Reviewer with a short summary (an adapted version of your Blurb) about your book, why you think it might be interesting for their readers, and a short back-story about your credibility as the author.

Ask them in which format they would like the review copy. This simple question guarantees you a *Yes* answer most of the time. Include a link to your Amazon page, but make it clear that you will 'gift' them a Kindle copy if they respond, or mail them a hard copy if they prefer.

Be aware that your hit-rate will be relatively low, depending on your sector, but be persistent. Never be afraid to send a second e-mail if you don't get a response within ten days or so. They may have been away on vacation, or sick, or one of any number of reasons why they missed your initial message.

Call Them. If you still get no response, pick up the phone and call them. You've *absolutely nothing to lose*. Your e-mail might have got stuck in a spam filter somewhere. They'll soon tell you if they're not interested, but this is part of the 'Hustle' so even if you hate being pushy on the phone, don't hesitate. You'll soon get the hang of it.

Remember this isn't about rejection; we've eliminated rejection by avoiding publishers and agents. This is about Marketing, and getting your masterpiece out to a wider audience. If you believe in your book, just go for it. Because if you get a review, you'll definitely get sales. *Recommendation*; another powerful Weapon of Influence! I've had reviews in niche publications turn into serialisations, and that can give you a great boost.

When you talk directly to a Reviewer, you're actually ahead of the big Publishers, who will have an Admin Staffer make these calls. In some niches, you may even get an interview out of it.

As with everything you do in Marketing, keep a log of your activities, and set reminders for yourself to follow up once the e-mails or letters go out. If you act like a professional author, people will treat you with respect and you may be surprised at some of the excellent contacts that you make, as well as the extra book sales you achieve.

15 – Adrenaline: Tracking Your Book Sales

Both Kindle and CreateSpace provide you with a useful on-screen dashboard, enabling you to track your sales day-by-day. Unfortunately, these two dashboards are not combined together, so you'll need to get used to using them separately.

Overview of the CreateSpace Dashboard

For CreateSpace, you'll need to log in each time you want to view your dashboard, but your browser will remember your login information so that all you have to do is click one button each time. You'll then be taken to your Member Dashboard where you can see your Projects, both finished and unfinished, add new titles as you write them, and see your unit sales in a month-to-date format. There's also a box on the dashboard that shows your running Royalty Balance, split by currency between the US, UK, and International markets.

Always remember when you're looking at your sales figures in CreateSpace, that any paperbacks that you've ordered through your Amazon Customer Account will show in up there, so don't get carried away with the numbers. There are various detailed royalty reports you can call up. CreateSpace updates very quickly, in fact so quickly that if you order five books for yourself, the number will crawl up one book at a time, which I can only assume means that the reporting system is connected to the printing machine itself, rather than the ordering system.

Overview of the KDP Dashboard

The KDP Dashboard is in a different format. Again you log in, probably with your Amazon account details; however the Kindle dashboard will stay open on your computer or tablet once you're logged in, but you'll need to refresh the window to see the most updated data.

Since mid 2014, the default display when you log in is a graph that will show you daily totals for your combined collection of titles. Bear in mind that these are *orders* rather than *sales*, and include books that are borrowed under the Kindle Owners Lending Library (KOLL) and Kindle Unlimited (KU), which will not usually register in your actual sales screens until the downloaded book has been opened and read past 10%.

You can use the drop-down boxes at the top to see the graph for each title, in each market, and over any period up to ninety days.

Above the graph are a number of options. The first option that it offers you is your *Bookshelf*, where you can see all your current titles, their US dollar list price, and their status. If you click on a title it will take you to the original information screens where you can add and change things like Keywords and Product Descriptions, and even upload a brand-new version of your Manuscript or Cover. You can also change your pricing, which will normally take somewhere between four and twelve hours to be reflected through to your Sales Page. It's very simple to use, once you've been through it the first time. Be aware that when you change a few things at once, some items (such as pricing) populate on Amazon quickly, whereas others (such as Cover Artwork) can take much longer because of the separate approval process they must pass through to ensure that you're working within the rules.

The *Reports* tab gives you the useful option to look at your Month-To-Date unit sales, which is the most interesting and exciting part of the process. When you open the tab you will see a list of each of your titles showing how many have been sold, returned, and borrowed. There's a separate report page for each of the geographical Amazon stores, and if you have selected *worldwide rights* for your book it's worth checking even the obscure ones every so often, because although the majority of your sales will made on Amazon.com and Amazon.co.uk, you may well see sales crop up on Amazon.ca (Canada) and even some of the European sites.

Units Borrowed – KDP Select & Kindle Unlimited

Just to remind you, when you uploaded your Kindle manuscript, you'll recall that you were given the option to enrol in KDP Select. One of the facilities that you enjoy if you enrol is that Kindle owners who are members of Amazon Prime are allowed to borrow one book free of charge each month, under the Kindle Owners Lending Library (KOLL) scheme. These books stay on their Kindle device for up to 30 days and then disappear. Amazon creates a fund each month and shares it amongst its authors, and it's not unusual to see $1.50 or $2.00 credited to your account for each time one of your books is borrowed. This seems like magic to you, the Author! No money changes hands, but you get paid for people borrowing your book.

There's no magic really, since Amazon Prime subscribers pay somewhere between $70 and $80 a year membership fee, and that's where the money comes from. Anecdotally, low-priced books don't usually register many borrows. However as your price increases, and the perceived relative value of a *borrow* grows, you may well see a substantial figure appearing in this column each month. My books are generally around the $3-$5 price range, and I see maybe 10% of my total royalties from KOLL borrowers each month.

More significant since mid-2014 is Kindle Unlimited (KU), which also shows in the dashboard, and will probably be a more significant number for most people. We covered KU and KOLL in detail earlier in the book (just in case you skipped that section).

Units Refunded

Inevitably, as you start to sell more books, you will see a few *Units Refunded* in your reports. If your book is of reasonable quality, and your Sales Page is honest and accurate, you shouldn't see very large numbers in this column. Amazon customers are allowed to return a Kindle book within seven days for a full refund. Surprisingly, this system is hardly ever abused, as evidenced by the low return numbers most authors experience. However, if you start to see numbers in excess of 5% each month, you should perhaps be examining whether your book is offering commensurate value, or if you have oversold on your Sales Page. Of course, some people simply make a mistake and buy the wrong book, so you really shouldn't worry about seeing two or three returns in every hundred sales.

If you're writing in the kids or young adult genres, you shouldn't be alarmed if you see higher return rates. The kids have clearly figured that, if they time it right, they can read and return a book without having to pay for it (for more than a few days) and they are masters at abusing the Amazon *no questions asked* system. Suck it up; we were all young once!

Other Reports

You will also see tabs for Promotions and Pre-Orders, which we already covered.

Tracking Methods

Monthly Tracking

For a casual author, it may be quite acceptable simply to wait for each month-end report (which actually appears about the 15th of the month following) just to see how much pocket money you've earned! However, if you're serious about your self-publishing, and you're aiming to publish more than one book, it's worth putting some tracking mechanisms in place early-on so that you can observe sales trends for your books. It's only by knowing how your book is selling that you'll understand when you need to make adjustments to things like price, promotion and your Sales Page elements.

Daily Tracking

Once you start moving up into selling hundreds of books per month, you might want to set up a daily tracking mechanism where you enter your sales into a spreadsheet or table at the end of every 24-hour period. You'll find that your daily sales numbers fluctuate quite widely but will usually trend on a daily average according to whatever happens in the first week of the month. If you're tracking daily, don't be disheartened if you drop well below your daily average from time to time, because you can reasonably expect some bumper days which will correct your trend. If you're interested in correlating your daily sales against your Sales Ranking, which you can see in your Amazon Sales Page, you can set this up in your spreadsheet and even build graphs and tables if you're so inclined. There is a comprehensive explanation about how to do this in "Make a Killing on Kindle" by Michael Alvear.

Personally, I am so excited to see how my books are doing that I usually check the Month-to-Date sales report at least three or four times a day, even though I know it doesn't update in real-time. Because I'm based in the UK, the numbers I see first thing in the morning often creep up quite nicely until lunchtime because of evening sales in the USA. So I check my daily tracking at midday each day. If I'm above my daily average, that gives me a little smile. If I'm below my daily average then I generally don't worry too much' because I figure it's going to pick up the next day or the day after, which it usually does.

Weekly Tracking

You will see on the KDP dashboard that the second set of reports you can access is your *Prior Six Weeks Royalties*, which is also segregated by market (.com,.co.uk and so on) and are updated each Sunday for the previous week. This will show you, week-by-week, how many books you sold of each title and the actual royalty you earned for each book. You'll probably notice that some of your books, particularly on Amazon.com, receive 70% royalties (which is what you selected when you set up your pricing), but some will only receive 35% royalties. This might confuse you at first, but the 35% royalty books are sold outside of the main Amazon.com markets. Unless you are writing for a particularly niche cultural or language market, these 35% sales will probably be in the minority. Of course, if you are running at a 99c or 99p promotional price, all your books will earn 35% for that period.

Once again, you may choose to transfer the data from these reports into a sales tracking spreadsheet of your own, in which case you can copy and paste the data, although you can't directly download these reports into Microsoft Excel. However, as of October 2014, Amazon has stated that they plan to withdraw this report. Instead you will be able to download an custom Excel report from the main screen (below the graph) instead. Both reports are running in parallel at the time of writing, but I expect to see the *Prior Six-Weeks Royalty* tab disappear any day now.

You'll find weekly tracking to be the most useful, because you can see trends based on the kinds of marketing and promotion you're doing. Don't get too worried if you see sales drop for a week, but if they start to drop for two or three weeks in succession, you should consider a price promotion or some other method of boosting them back up, such as buying a "gig" in fiverr.com.

The worst thing that can happen if you successfully get on the first page on an Amazon Search is that your sales drop away without you doing anything about it, because eventually you will drop off the first page. Just as Amazon's momentum will carry you up when you're rising, it will also carry you down and withdraw its support if you are falling for too long. For this reason, if you're serious about making money from your writing, you really need to be tracking at least weekly in the main markets for all your titles.

Royalty Reports

The third type of report which is available from the KDP dashboard is the *Prior Months Royalties* report which arrives around about the 15th of each month. These can be downloaded easily into Microsoft Excel although they're not that easy to automatically manipulate, because some months you may sell in some of the more obscure markets, which means that your Excel lines are never the same from one month to the next. However, if you're familiar with Excel, or even if you're not, you should be able to figure out how to analyse these reports, and compare your sales month-to-month.

I find graphs in Excel to be the best way to do this. Waiting a month to find out how you're doing is not the greatest, so this is no substitute for tracking week by week. However, the monthly reports give you a complete breakdown, including the royalties you receive for books that were borrowed under KOLL and KU. The monthly report shows you exactly how much you're going to get paid when Amazon gets around to sending you some money. Just for your information, royalties are usually paid around two months in arrears.

Your Sales Rankings

On your Sales page, you'll see your book's Sales Ranking. It's at the bottom of the block of data just below the Sales Description panel. There you will see your position in the overall Kindle Paid Rankings (or 'Books' if you're looking at your Paperback Sales Page separately). For the purpose of this exercise, we're going to ignore your 'Books' ranking, because it's most likely that you will only be selling a minority of your work through traditional books. Most of your sales, and most of your money, are going to come from your Kindle e-book downloads.

Amazon does not publish the data about how many books constitute a specific Kindle ranking, however there's lots of amateur data out there which suggest that a ranking below 10,000 indicates sales of less than 10 books a day, and below 50,000 equates to less than one book a day. Remember, this is store-specific, so your ranking on Amazon.com is completely unrelated to your ranking on (say) Amazon.co.uk, which is a much smaller market. My own experience in the

UK market is that a book ranked below 10,000 is selling less than three copies a day.

Once you break into the top 10,000, which is my own personal target for each book I publish, you'll be starting to earn some interesting royalties on .com. Even in the lower reaches of the top 10k, you'll be moving anything up to 500 units a month, and if you're making $2 each time, you're soon into four-figure months. If you have ambitions to make a living at this, you'll need five or six books performing at that level before you can give the finger to the Man! If you can crack the top 5000, you're starting to see more than a thousand downloads a month, and if you can write books that pull in that kind of cash, you should think about going full-time just as fast as you can!

Your overall Sales Ranking fluctuates wildly through the day, because Amazon (allegedly) updates every hour. So you should set up a method of tracking your 'best' daily ranking, by going into the site every hour and making a note of it.

Hah! I'm joking, of course! Nobody has time to do this, so here's a way to automate it.

Go to www.kindlenationdaily.com and set up a (free) account. Then you can go into their *E-Book Tracker*, which is very easy and self-explanatory, and set up tracking for each of your books, and any other books (competitors, for example) that you want to track. Once you're set up, the system will track any book's highest and lowest daily sales ranking and display it in a list and a graph, so you can see exactly what's happening. It only tracks Amazon.com, by the way.

The UK Market

In the UK market, the numbers are smaller, but quality material has less competition. Although I cannot imagine why any self-publishing author would limit himself or herself only to publishing in the USA (and Australia, NZ, South Africa), apparently there are whole sectors of the Kindle Book market which simply don't cross the Atlantic Ocean. If you're UK based, and promoting primarily in your home market, it's much easier to get ranked higher on Amazon.co.uk, and as we know, the higher you rank, the more visible you are, the more books you sell, and the higher you rank.

Top 10,000 in Kindle Paid Rankings in the UK equates to around 6 books a day. Top 5000 is about double that. As we already know, the Amazon stores and their respective rankings are completely separate, so if you're a UK author, or even if you aren't, if you can get momentum and visibility in the UK market, you can be a bigger fish in a smaller but still capacious pool, in a much shorter time.

Category Rankings

Whereas your overall Ranking is a nice measure of your general progress, it actually doesn't do much for your Sales unless you break into the Top 100, when of course you will join a completely new search category and the sky above you will change colour completely! If you're a fiction author, you'll already be aware that the vast majority if the Top 100 are novels (rather than non-fiction) and those that aren't are usually biographies. What you may not know is that around 25% of all books in the Top 100 (All Paid) at any given moment are debut or self-published, so you have a good chance if you have a great book and you can light a fire under your sales. This book is not intended to show you how to do that: there are many other books out there that claim to be able to help you, but if it were that easy everyone would be doing it.

If you're minded to commit to serious investment when launching your book (once you have cast-iron proof that it's good), then you might consider approaching a specialist PR consultant. It won't come cheap, but if you keep hold of your rights and you can get a groundswell going on Amazon, you could become very rich indeed. Infiltrating book clubs, getting mainstream press reviews, and all these tactics will drive your profile. But, to repeat, if your book isn't world-class, you'll struggle to reach such lofty heights!.

For the non-fiction Author, the chances of breaking into the Top 100 are virtually non-existent (unless you've genuinely written that Alchemy classic about how to turn lead pipes into gold bars), but there are significant compensations. First and foremost, you can probably charge more money for your book than the novelist, especially in the early days. Secondly, you can probably turn out ten or twelve books a year, against the novelist's one or two, and if you pick your subjects carefully, most of them will sell OK.

But, most importantly, you can quite easily get your book onto the first page in your Category Search. This is the Weapon of Influence which drives non-fiction writing. If you're showing up on the front page, especially the top row, of any Category Search screen, you're on display to every qualified buyer who is actually looking for your subject. The odds of a sale are very good indeed. And the more you sell, the stronger your presence becomes and the longer you'll stay at the top of the heap, adding Relevance, and accruing Ranking points.

As I explained earlier, one of the first books I published has been the Number One Bestseller in its category since two weeks after publication. I hustled to get it there, infiltrating niche Facebook pages and forums, and using various tactics to gain momentum, but since it arrived there, no-one has challenged it (apart from the occasional Free Promotion). I do absolutely nothing to that book now, and it consistently sells more than two hundred downloads and fifty paperbacks every month. I have never offered it for free, and I have never priced it below the 70% royalty threshold. The broad Category Search returns 438 results. It sells, so it stays at the top of the first page, both on Relevance and Popularity, and just keeps selling. In addition, the main keyword (which is also the title) was a popular search term I found in the Google Keywords tool, so it shows up on the first page of Google and drives more traffic to its Amazon Sales Page. I must add that the book is pretty good, as evidenced by the Average Reviews, although I have a couple of one stars on there too!

This demonstrates the power of Category Rankings in niches, and the smaller markets like UK. The virtuous circle takes us back to the original concepts in Section One for non-fiction: try to choose a category where you have some expertise and where there is a steady flow of customers, and use all the tools at your disposal to drive your book up to the most visible place, Page One, in its Category Search.

Because that's where you really want to be!

16 - And Finally

There, you did it! By now, you either know what I know, or you're outselling me! I hope this book has equipped you with the tools you need to make a go of your writing, and earn some money into the bargain.

When I first started writing for Amazon, I played at it for a few months. I would drift around the house until lunch-time and finally sit down at my computer around two in the afternoon. Once the first book started to sell, I started to do the mental calculations about how hard I would have to work and how long it would take me to replace my fat-cat executive salary with book royalties. Here's what I figured:

This is a numbers game. Provided you can keep the good ideas coming, and put in the hours on the keyboard, you just replicate the winning formula and the royalties keep increasing. You may start by moving four or five books a day, and then you see it build, month by month, as you launch another book, do some promotion, get some reviews, and grow. The writing gets faster because you become more organized and disciplined. And once you see that your Marketing 'Hustle' gets results, you'll have a formula that you can replicate each time. Before you know it, you're shifting twenty, thirty, forty books a day, and then you can see your first hundred-book day appearing over the horizon.

I could write shorter books, and I could spend less time editing the quality, but that just wouldn't feel good. You should never deliver anything less than the best product you can create, not only because the reviewers will find you out, but also because you want to be proud of your work.

Now, I find I'm always working on some aspect of my book business. I start earlier in the mornings, and write or edit at least six hours every day. In the evenings I'm on the sofa in front of the TV, but the iPad is always in my hand, either reading and reviewing other author's books, or working on my Marketing Hustle! None of it's a chore, because it all adds up to the most enjoyable job I ever had, and I hope you'll soon feel this way too.

I promised you some recommendations of other books you might read if you want to go deeper into some of the more advanced Amazon Marketing techniques. You'll find these listed in the Resources section, as well as a list of Facebook Groups that you can investigate. I would encourage you to use every tool at your disposal to drive your Writing and Marketing, because if you don't do it, plenty of others will!

Finally, *please, please,* (see; I'm not too proud to beg) Review this book on Amazon if you found it useful. **Please do it now**, it'll only take a few minutes of your time. Otherwise you might get so busy you'll forget. I promise that if you e-mail me when your book is launched, I'll do the same for you!

You can e-mail me directly on;

ricksmith@marketaccess.tv

Or better still, send me a Facebook Friend Request to **Rick Smith Author**. I have hundreds of independent self-published authors on my Facebook Friend List, and they'll be only too happy to collaborate with you if you have a quality book to launch.

I also run workshops from time to time, in the UK and South Africa. If this interests you, you'll find details and dates at www.spmasterclass.com

And, even after reading this book, you still feel that you need some extra help, take a look at www.ricksmithbooks.com and you may find what you're looking for, in terms of formatting, cover creation, editing services, or the full publishing service. I work with a great team of outsourced specialist freelancers, whom I trust to do a good job; so don't hesitate to ask if you need some help.

Good Luck, Write Well, and Prosper!

Rick

Additional Resources

Books You Should Read

There are literally thousands of Self-Publishing guides in the market. Pretty much every self-published author writes one at some stage, and many of them are decidedly average, or at the very least repetitive. I should know; I've read them all.

This list is by no means exhaustive as far as the good ones go, but if you only read these books, you would have covered around 99% of the information that's out there.

Platform by Michael Hyatt

Hyatt is a massively successful Social Media Strategy blogger with a huge following. This seminal book lays out strategies to build a far-reaching platform which can be harnessed to deliver a willing audience for anything you write. There are some grand concepts in here, and not all of it is useful, however a new Author will find some great observations on human nature in general and consumer behaviour in particular.

Make Your Book Work Harder by Nancy Hendrickson & Michelle Campbell-Scott

I keep Nancy and Michelle's fantastic book permanently in the top row of my Kindle Library on my iPad, because there's barely a week goes by that I don't feel the need to consult it. This book is packed full of great advice for Indie Authors, such as how to get on to other e-book platforms, how to do an audiobook with ACX, and some really cool stuff abut Social Media campaigns and Book Promotion opportunities.

Make a Killing on Kindle by Michael Alvear

For me, this is one of the best books currently in print about Book Marketing for independent authors. Michael Alvear is a successful Amazon author in his own right, and this book will give you many great tactics to drive your sales, with not much effort and zero cost. A must-read.

Createspace and Kindle Self-Publishing Matrix by Chris Naish

If you really want to drill down into keyword strategies, this book is the blueprint. I must admit a bias here, because Chris Naish used my book as the central case study when he was formulating his Matrix (he calls me Agent Smith). If you like the analytical approach to marketing, this is the book for you. If you get keywords right, your book will do things you never expected.

The Kindle Publishing Bible by Tom Corson-Knowles

Corson-Knowles is one of the new gurus of the self-publishing business, and all his books are worthy of your attention. This one leads with some great advice on titles and keywords, and lots of solid Marketing advice for newcomers.

Pictures on Kindle by Aaron Shepard

Aaron is undoubtedly my favourite Author Geek, and all his technical books are worth their weight in gold when you're learning your way around Kindle publishing. This one is particularly noteworthy because it completely demystifies the process of getting pictures and graphics to display well on all Kindle devices, which is far from simple. He also has two others I would recommend: *From Word to Kindle,* and *HTML Fixes for Kindle.* Pure gold.

Is *99c the New Free?* by Steve Scott

Scott is another of the well-known gurus in this market, and this book, a relatively recent publication, gives a great explanation of why 99c pricing is better for your business than free promotion, and how to use it effectively.

Facebook Groups

There are lots of Authors and Self-Publishers' Facebook Groups which you can choose from. Some of the better ones are real thriving communities for independents like you, and there you can learn advanced techniques very quickly, ask questions, and generally interact with experienced authors who are usually only too happy to pass on what they know. Try to avoid Groups that only seem to have pages of self-promotion, particularly for free books, because these will clog up your Newsfeed with useless stuff.

Two which I recommend are as follows:

The Fab Friday 99 Cents Promotion Group for Authors https://www.facebook.com/groups/200905610068048/ and

Kindle Publishing Bible -- https://www.facebook.com/groups/KindlePublishers/

These are closed groups, and you will need to apply to join. However, they contain quality people and the moderators ensure that junk promotional material never makes it to the main feed.

And here is a more complete list:

Pat's First Kindle Book -- https://www.facebook.com/groups/357112331027292/
99 cent Kindle Deals -- https://www.facebook.com/groups/215681398501172/

99¢ Kindle Book Promotion --
https://www.facebook.com/groups/198597020319359/
Page One Profits Kindle Group --
https://www.facebook.com/groups/pageoneprofits/
Author's Forum --
https://www.facebook.com/groups/AuthorsForum01/
Self Publish Bootcamp --
https://www.facebook.com/groups/selfpublishbootcamp/
Wicked Simple K --
https://www.facebook.com/groups/387202538033195/
Author Meeting Place --
https://www.facebook.com/groups/authormeetingplace/
Authors, Agents, and Aspiring Writers --
https://www.facebook.com/groups/204725947524/
Author Exchange --
https://www.facebook.com/groups/200396383343774/
Writers' Group --
https://www.facebook.com/groups/memberswritersgroup/
The Literary Lounge --
https://www.facebook.com/groups/135486133130440/
Literary Discussion Group – We promote ourselves --
https://www.facebook.com/groups/AuthorsAndReviews/
Books, Books, and more Books!!! --
https://www.facebook.com/groups/320356974732142/
Kindle Publishers --
https://www.facebook.com/groups/512098985483106/
Ebook Review Club --
https://www.facebook.com/groups/123094781181179/
Kindle Marketing Revelations Insiders
https://www.facebook.com/groups/kindlemarketingrevelati
ons/
Authors Promoting Authors --
https://www.facebook.com/groups/apablog/
Book Promotion --

https://www.facebook.com/groups/BookPromotion/
Next Top Author --
https://www.facebook.com/groups/nexttopauthor/
Kindle Publishing Bible --
https://www.facebook.com/groups/KindlePublishers/
Marketing for Authors --
https://www.facebook.com/groups/146813612165228/

The Fab Friday 99 Cents Promotion Group for Authors
https://www.facebook.com/groups/200905610068048/

Free Book Promotion Sites

This list is too long to include here, so if you are really committed to Free Promotions, particularly if you are a new Fiction Author, simply Google "Free Book Promotion Sites" and you'll get a massive list. If you are going this way, plan carefully, and blitz all the lists on one day. If you do it thoroughly, you will get thousands of downloads. However, you may not see these convert to Sales in the longer term, so balance your Effort versus Return and make sure you know what you are trying to achieve.

Finally, please send me a Facebook Friend Request on Rick Smith Author, and join a group of happy and industrious independent self-published authors who are always looking out for the opportunity to help one another succeed.

Subscribe to my Self-Publishing Masterclass Newsletter and Download "Stunning Covers" for Free

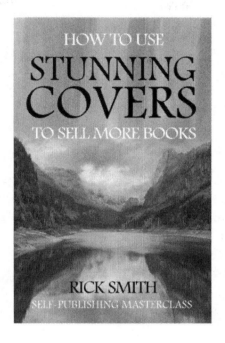

Just Click or Copy the Link: http://tiny.cc/wc84gx

WRITE FAST, BEAT PROCRASTINATION

MILE-HIGH WORD COUNT

& WRITING PRODUCTIVITY

HOW TO CRUNCH 5000 WORDS A DAY, EVERY DAY

Rick Smith

CreateSpace & Kindle Self-Publishing Masterclass

Write Fast, Write More, Beat Procrastination and Finish Your Book.

Nobody can buy your book until you finish writing it. Nothing happens until you publish. If you're struggling to get it done, maybe you need a System!

Perhaps you're already an Author, but you need a competitive edge. You need to write more books, and that takes time. Whatever the case, maybe you're holding yourself back:

- Do you struggle with procrastination and getting started each day?

- Are you easily distracted from your writing?

- With all your other responsibilities, is finding enough time to write a problem for you?

In *'Mile-High Word-Count'*, the latest Self-Publishing Masterclass from Bestselling Author Rick Smith, you'll discover proven systems and techniques that will supercharge your writing productivity:

- Secrets of the Five Hour Author: Write a new book every month in only 5 Hours a Week.

- The HITs Writing System: High-Intensity Interval Training for ambitious Authors.

- The Lean-Mean 5:2 Author: Write like a whirlwind for just 45 minutes a day: and take the Weekends off!

- The Mile-High Word-Count: 5000+ Words a day in only Four Weeks!

You'll also learn the *Secret Weapons* that will double or treble your Productivity when you're writing a book.

- 14 Top Tips to Beat Procrastination.

- 5 Simple Kick-Start methods that will make you Want To Write every day.

- Where to find amazing FREE Software that makes planning and organizing easy.

You could spend months or years trying to write faster, or you could learn all you need to know in a weekend in *"Mile High Word-Count"*. The book business is booming, but it's also highly competitive. Join the Winners; Leave Nothing to Chance.

Just search for Rick Smith on the Amazon bookstore.

Made in the USA
San Bernardino, CA
26 November 2016